A Special Gift

A Special Gift

A Devotional for Mothers
of Children with Differences

Carrie T. Gruman-Trinkner

OLIVER
NELSON

THOMAS NELSON PUBLISHERS
Nashville

Unless otherwise noted, Scripture quotations are from THE NEW KING JAMES VERSION. Copyright © 1979, 1980, 1982, Thomas Nelson, Inc., Publishers.

Scripture quotations noted NIV are from the HOLY BIBLE: NEW INTERNATIONAL VERSION®. Copyright © 1973, 1978, 1984 by International Bible Society. Used by permission of Zondervan Publishing House. All rights reserved.

The devotion "This Gift Is Small . . . Does It Have Any Impact?" appeared in slightly different format in *Side By Side*, a devotional published by Christ the Rock Community Church, 1999.

Some names have been changed to protect the privacy of certain individuals.

Library of Congress Cataloging-in-Publication Data

Gruman-Trinkner, Carrie T.
    A Special Gift: A Devotional for Mothers of Children With Differences / Carrie T. Gruman-Trinkner.
      p. cm.
    ISBN 0-7852-6805-7
    1. Mothers of exceptional children—Prayer-books and devotions—English. I. Title
BV4847 .G78 2000
242'.6431—dc21

                                     99–059103
                                     CIP

Printed in the United States of America

1 2 3 4 5 6 BVG 05 04 03 02 01 00

For I know the thoughts that I think toward you, says the LORD, thoughts of peace and not of evil, to give you a future and a hope.

—Jeremiah 29:11

To Aiden:
My precious son and God's perfect gift

Acknowledgments

Thanks to my own little ones: Kaitlynne, Aaron, Alex, Kelsey, and Aiden—your lives fill me with joy! To my extended family for their belief in this work: Tom and Eileen Gruman, Mark and Katie, Ray and Sherry, Bernadette and George, Mary and Craig, and all their little ones who make life so fun; The Writer's Institute at UW-Madison, Wisconsin: Marshall J. Cook, Christine DeSmet, and Laurel Yourke for helping make dreams reality; Scott Edelstein for his patient instruction; those who saw early my future vocation: Brenda Wilkolm Dennison, Mary Werth, and Mary Dalles; James Geneske, Jackie Gyrion, Reverend John and Pat Poppe, and Kim McKeown for their help in gathering the beautiful stories included in this book; Heidi Teal, Aiden's beloved speech therapist and friend; Christ the Rock Community Church—especially Pastor Bill Lenz, Pastor Dave VandeHey, and Pastor John Kieffer, and all who prayed and supported our family through times of crisis; Jody Giordana for her faithfulness to Aiden; the Cleft-Palate team at UW-Hospitals and Clinics, especially Dr. Steven Hardy; Jan "Ma" Lenz for her love, prayers, and servanthood during Aiden's first two years; and Ben Lenz for beginning the healing process.

With deepest love and gratitude to the Lord who gifted me with Aiden and equipped and empowered me, blessing me beyond measure.

The Baby You Hold

Congratulations on the birth of your special baby! I rejoice with you at the miracle of new birth. You hold in your arms an image-bearer of God. Your child has been placed here with you for a purpose—you have been gifted with a special child.

I also sympathize with the mix of emotions you are feeling today. Along with joy and relief, you are probably experiencing fear, confusion, anger, and perhaps even guilt. You may wonder if you have done something to cause this child to have differences from other children. You may wonder if God is somehow punishing you through your child's problems.

Let me assure you first that God does not "punish" us by harming children—not ever. God's perfect plan called for perfect babies. However, we live in a fallen world where perfection is absent. Thus, you hold a less-than-perfect child. And I will point out that every baby—every one, with no exception—is less than perfect.

God weeps with you at the sorrow you feel. He knows your fears and longs to comfort you. He loves both you and that wonderful new creature you hold.

Inside the covers of this book, I offer you God's hope and love through His Word, the stories of other mothers who share your pain, and short prayers that may help you talk to God about your situation.

Only God, the One who loves you and suffers with you, can

heal the broken heart you are now experiencing. Reach out to Him—He longs to hold you and lead you beyond this present darkness and into the light of His love and care.

I pray that you will find not only comfort and strength, but also a richer relationship with the Lord who will sustain you and your child through the times ahead.

Celebrate Your Baby

Rejoice in the Lord always. Again I will say, rejoice!
—Philippians 4:4

Never lose sight of the fact that you have been given a wondrous new creation—a baby—to love and hold and care for. Your baby may have some flaws . . . but don't we all have flaws?

Joanne Green, a woman who adopted three beautiful children with facial differences, once wisely told me to always remember that "the baby you hold is a baby *first*, and cleft-affected second!"

How right she is! Many people had a difficult time looking at Aiden's disfigured face, gasping at the first sight. My first look at him was frightening too.

But then I saw those incredible eyes gazing calmly into my own. I fell absolutely in love! He was my child, the blessing God had entrusted to my care.

Yes, Aiden needs more than a dozen surgeries, extensive orthodontic work, speech therapy, and other not-so-pleasant challenges. But he is funny and bright and loving.

He is the first of my five children to love snuggling on my lap for extended periods of time. He charms others with his ready smile, crooked though it might be. He has a deep belly laugh that is irresistibly contagious. At the age of eighteen months, he has already learned an extensive vocabulary in sign language. (His palate construction is not complete, and he cannot form most consonants.) He has the most expressive blue eyes I have ever seen. Every child in our neighborhood adores this fair-haired toddler.

If I dwell on his future surgeries, I feel defeated and angry. But when I see the wonderful boy he is becoming, I rejoice. I thank God that He gifted me with this precious son. Aiden has taught me to accept and to love, no matter the situation. All of my children have learned to be compassionate and respectful of anyone with differences.

Aiden is reason to rejoice. So is your baby. Hang a sign, have a party, take his or her portrait, send out announcements! Rejoice—God has given you a precious and wondrous gift— one that will touch your heart forever.

Prayer: Lord, focus my eyes on the beauty of this child You have placed in my hands. Thank You for this little life. Help me to rejoice in the wonderful traits of my child and what he can teach me.

He Is Close

The LORD is near to those who have a broken heart.

—Psalm 34:18

Your heart is broken. How do you handle the pain of knowing your child faces challenges that others will never face? Where can you turn to lift this crushing heaviness? Who is there to comfort you in your loneliness? Is there anyone who understands?

Yes, dear mother. The Lord is here. He is close. He sees your pain. He longs to embrace you in His loving arms, to comfort you and to restore your joy.

Take a moment of rest. Close your eyes and surrender your mind to Him. Feel His love wrap around you. Know that He is close. Know that He is in control and that it will be OK. No matter the circumstance, no matter the outcome, He will be there to love you through it.

Let Him be your *strength*—you don't have to do it on your own.
Let Him be your *rest*—He will refresh your exhausted soul.
Let Him be your *comfort*—He will ease your pain.
Let Him be your *guide*—He will lead you into the future.
Let Him be your *companion*—He will never leave you.
Let Him be your *joy*—He will fill your heart with singing.

You are not alone. The Lord has many hearts on this earth willing to spend time with you, to help you cope with the stress . . . and the housework. Call upon the Lord's people—contact a local church and let them know your situation. Do not be afraid.

You are not alone. There are millions of us in the United States who have children with differences. Contact one of us. Call your local hospital, mental health agencies, or look in the telephone book for support groups in your area. Many support groups can also be found on the Internet. Know that we pray for you when we lift prayers for others in our situation.

You are not alone. The Lord *Himself* is near.

Prayer: Lord, help me to know You are near. Thank You for Your promise to remain close to those whose hearts are broken. Thank You for being my strength, my rest, my comfort, my guide, my companion, and my joy.

Permission to Wrestle with God

Then Jacob was left alone; and a Man wrestled with him until the breaking of day . . . So Jacob called the name of the place Peniel: "For I have seen God face to face, and my life is preserved."
—Genesis 32:24, 30

Many of us are under the false understanding that we should never, ever voice our displeasure to God. You may have been taught that it is wrong to be angry, or that a *good* girl should always be accepting of whatever may befall her.

We see in the book of Genesis that Jacob did indeed wrestle with God. He wrestled all night long in a desperate battle. In the end, Jacob begged for a blessing and received it.

Have you taken the time to wrestle with God? Have you told Him how upset you are that your baby is not "perfect"? Have you told Him of the anger you feel over the pain that your child must endure—whether it be physical or emotional? Have you told Him that it isn't fair that your child has differences?

God knows it isn't fair. He knows your anger. He not only gives you permission to express it to Him, but He invites you to do so.

Take some time. Go for a drive. Walk in the woods. Have your spouse or a friend watch the baby while you wander through a silent house. And talk out loud. Tell God your fears, your anger, your pain. Yell, scream, cry, and reach out.

God is big enough to hear it. He can handle it.

You were never designed to hold it all inside. You are a relational being—created for relationship with God. And what healthy relationship can thrive unless we are honest and open with one another?

And once you have expressed yourself, sit quietly. Allow God to touch your heart with His healing balm. Let His peace restore you and strengthen you.

Never be afraid to go to Him, no matter what you are feeling, no matter how many times you must express it. He is there, always, for you.

Prayer: Lord, thank You that I can always come to You. Thank You for Your understanding ear and compassionate heart. Help me to always be open with You about my thoughts and feelings.

Taking a Chance on Trusting

> *Trust in the LORD with all your heart,*
> *And lean not on your own understanding;*
> *In all your ways acknowledge Him,*
> *And He shall direct your paths.*
> —Proverbs 3:5–6

Across the highway from my house, two red-tailed hawks took up residence in a towering tree. I could sit in my living room and look across our balcony to watch the hawks build their massive nest. Stick by stick they painstakingly constructed it.

Finally, one day, there appeared three eggs in the nest. (With my home on a hill above the highway, I had the vantage point to look into the nest with binoculars.) Patiently, the female hawk tended the nest. Her mate hovered nearby, coaxing her from the nest, periodically, to soar into the sky. At long last the eggs hatched. I watched as the babies grew fuzz and then feathers. Their greedy mouths kept their parents busy. Frantically, the parents would search for food. I covered our rabbits in the backyard, fearing they, too, would soon be supper for those baby hawks.

Soon, by some God-ordained order, the mother hawk knew the time had come to send her babies out on their own. They perched on the edge of the nest, teetering in what seemed to be fear. Trusting their mother, they eased themselves over the edge of the nest. I watched in horror as the first plummeted earthward. Suddenly, the little hawk spread its wings and began to soar. The mother joined it. Soon all four birds were effortlessly skating across the sky.

The mother hawk did not know the physics of flight. She did not discuss the procedure with her young. She just did her job as a mother and, without understanding, allowed the Lord to direct her path.

So it is with us. As loving parents, we build our "nests," preparing for our baby. We tend her and nurture her, all the while gently pushing her to achieve the God-ordained plan for her life.

The mother hawk had to trust that her young would fly. She prepared them, gently pushed them, and then left the flying to the hand of God.

We must trust that God, who cares for the hawk, will also care for our babies. We simply provide for them and teach them as God molds them into the person He desires them to become.

Our children may be more limited in their accomplishments than some, but that is OK. God will direct their paths—and ours—no matter what they may be, so long as we trust those paths to Him.

Prayer: Lord, I may not understand the path You have set before me, but I trust You to lead me. I ask that You teach me to trust You with all my heart.

Blessed Are Those Who Trust the Lord

> For he shall be like a tree planted by the waters,
> Which spreads out its roots by the river,
> And will not fear when heat comes.
> —Jeremiah 17:8

One summer a tornado swept its tail through our backyard. The house was not harmed, nor were those of us in it. But in the early morning hours, as we stepped outside to survey the damage, I saw that two massive shade trees had been pulled up by the roots and tossed aside like twigs.

I loved those trees. My children had climbed them. They had provided shade and added beauty to our yard.

We cut them up, carted them away, and filled the huge holes with dirt, leaving the lawn with a yawning gap where they had once stood. Silly as it may seem, I grieved the loss of those trees. They had seemed so strong and healthy, seemingly able to withstand anything. All summer I tended the yard, planting flowers, mowing . . . and missing my trees. We had a young family, so replacing those huge trees was financially impossible.

Winter came and passed. And one earthy spring day, I walked into the yard and stopped short. There, in the dirt where our trees had stood, were sprouts—the trees were growing back! All summer I watched them reach upward, stretching and rising into the air.

Now they stand once again in the yard. They survived that tornado, rested one winter, and came back renewed. They aren't quite the same as before, but they survived. And they have much to offer my children in the future: shade, beauty, and a place to climb.

Are you in the midst of the tornado? Are the difficulties facing you and your child threatening to destroy you? Trust in the Lord, send out your roots—reach out to Him. Let Him give you the rest and renewal your soul needs.

Just like the trees that we had thought were destroyed, you will survive to rise again with the Lord's help. And you will have much to offer others through your life experience.

Prayer: Lord, in the midst of the tornado, help me to see that the storm will ebb. Life will become sane once again, and You will guide the way. Thank You for Your gift of rest and renewal.

A Time to Refresh

And He said to them, "Come aside by yourselves to a deserted place and rest a while."

—Mark 6:31

In today's frantic world, it can be easy to overlook the necessity of quiet time to reflect, pray, and commune with God.

There is so much to do, so many things that demand our time and attention. And parenting a child with differences can be an especially overwhelming situation. And yet, even in the midst of their ministry, Jesus called His disciples aside to be refreshed and renewed by spending time alone with Him.

Therese had three young children when her fourth child was born. Keegan had several interruptions in his physical development. As a result, he was unable to eat properly. Therese spent hours trying to feed her infant a minute amount of formula. Eventually he needed a feeding tube.

Alongside the demand this put on Therese's limited time, her other children needed her. So did her husband. So did her house. As she struggled through each day, she fell further and further behind. And Therese became more and more frustrated, prone to snapping at the children and her husband. She felt as though she were drowning in an endless whirlpool of activity—all of it *necessary!*

A turning point came one morning as she was cleaning Keegan's feeding tube. Her five-year-old daughter rushed in, excited with a ladybug she had found in the backyard. Therese jumped, spilling the warm water. "How many times do I have to tell you to leave me alone when I am working with Keegan?" she yelled. Immediately her heart lurched as her daughter turned away, her eyes brimming with tears.

That evening, Therese and her husband sat down and came up with a respite plan. Therese would spend one half hour each night with her Bible while her husband took over the chores. She would take one evening a week to leave the house and spend time with other believers in a Bible study.

Within only two weeks, Therese discovered the strength that comes from spending restful time with the Lord. She felt refreshed and able to cope with the stresses of raising a child with differences. She no longer snapped in frustration at her other children, and she didn't feel exhausted.

Her time didn't magically increase, and her chores didn't decrease. But Therese found the key to reviving her soul—time with the Lord.

Prayer: Lord, in the midst of the whirlpool, You are a lifesaver. Help me to commit my time to daily fellowship with You.

All Alone—Who Can Understand?

> *Then she called the name of the LORD who spoke to her, You-Are-the-God-Who-Sees; for she said, "Have I also here seen Him who sees me?"*
>
> —Genesis 16:13

After years of unfulfilled promises, Sarai gave her handmaiden, Hagar, to Abram. Finding herself pregnant with Abram's child, Hagar began to despise her mistress, causing Sarai to treat her badly. When Hagar fled from Sarai's mistreatment, she found herself all alone in the desert.

Can you imagine what was going through her mind? Did she wish for death? Undoubtedly, she felt all alone in her misery, sure that no one could understand, let alone help. Her situation must have seemed desperate and hopeless.

And yet, One did come who understood. He saw this runaway and comforted her with a promise and a command. He told her to return, that she would bear a son who would give her descendants that would be too numerous to count.

Hagar came to the awesome realization that God did *see* her—that one seemingly insignificant girl and her problems did indeed matter to Him. She named Him El Roi, "the God Who Sees."

Those of us who parent a child with differences often feel like Hagar: alone, misunderstood, and afraid. Our situation may seem as hopeless and as desperate as Hagar's. Or we may be struggling with a lesser burden—a situation still full of difficulty no matter the degree. As we toil through difficult and lonely days with sometimes heavy hearts, we can be comforted in knowing that there is a God who *sees* us, understanding our situation as no other possibly can.

Take heart, mother, and know that God sees. You are never alone.

Prayer: Lord, thank You for the eyes that never close in sleep. Watch over me and my child, surround us with Your mindful presence, and help us to remember that You are always there.

This Gift Is Small . . .
(Does It Have Any Impact?)

All the believers were together and had everything in common . . . they gave to anyone as he had need.

—Acts 2:44–45 NIV

Need—real need—can sometimes strike without warning.

It was during such a time that I learned the blessing of a giving and loving church. My fifth child was born horribly disfigured with no roof in his mouth, a gum line split open in two places and pushed forward to resemble a duck's bill, and virtually no upper lip.

Reeling from shock, I left my son in the hospital that first Sunday to attend Christ the Rock, my home church for the previous seven years. My tears flowed both in grief and gratitude as I listened to hundreds of voices pray for the well-being of my child.

In the following days I learned that the Body doesn't just give lip service—their commitment came alive, as one after another, my brothers and sisters stopped in with gifts of food, money, and time. My laundry was done, my house was cleaned, our muddy back porch area received a new cement slab, and my children were cared for . . . as I struggled to feed a baby who could only eat one-quarter ounce of milk in one hour.

During Aiden's subsequent surgeries, the church again stepped forward to baby-sit and provide meals. Cards, letters, and prayers continued as our family slowly became able to cope.

I know that many of the church family were giving out of their own need. Their gifts and prayers combined to strengthen us as a family, caused God to bless us abundantly, and allowed us, in turn, to reach out to other families *throughout the nation* who are grieving the loss of the "perfect child."

When we give sacrificially from the heart, we reap a harvest beyond human belief and description. Learning to accept these blessings has been, in itself, one of the greatest blessings of all.

Prayer: Lord, help me to understand that, through Your power, any small offering can be combined with those of others and increased to overflowing. May I never be ashamed to give out of my need and to receive from Your abundant stores, no matter the size of the gift.

God Sees Beyond the Differences

God does not judge by external appearance.

Galatians 2:6 NIV

I have a portrait of my son and me that stands framed in our living room. It was taken two days before Aiden's first surgery to reconstruct his face. My friend Theresa took the picture. I am wearing a white nightgown; Aiden is naked and wrapped in soft, gauzy cloth. He lies facing me in my arms. His legs are tucked against my stomach. His hands are folded together under his chin as though he were praying. He is just beginning to smile. The smile hasn't touched his mouth yet, but you can see it clearly in his eyes—in the way they shine up at me. I am laughing in the picture, enjoying my wonderful little boy.

The picture may not seem beautiful to many. They would probably see the huge holes beneath each of his nostrils, the piece of gum that protrudes outward like a little duck bill, and the flattened, distended nose.

No, most people would probably miss the beauty of that

little boy gazing up adoringly at his mommy. They wouldn't know of his ready smile and deep laughter. They wouldn't think of his sweet smell and soft skin.

They would see a face that is different. And they would miss something wonderful.

God doesn't rest His eyes on the differences of our children. He doesn't look at His people and judge their beauty in human terms. He sees the wonder and beauty *within* each one of us.

As you come to know your baby, you, too, will see all the remarkable things about him or her. That difference in your baby that initially may have shocked you—whether it is physically apparent or not—will fade into the background for you. It may still be present, and you may need to address it on a daily or hourly basis, but it will become secondary to the incredible little person you love.

People rarely notice the thin scars under Aiden's nose now. What they do notice is his use of sign language. That may frighten some at first, but once they look closer, with their hearts—just as God does—all of that slips away.

What they see is an image-bearer of the almighty God, a precious and gifted little boy with soft blond hair, sparkling blue eyes, and a ready smile.

Prayer: Lord, it is a blessing to know You look beyond our appearance and see our value in whom we have been created to be. Help me to see beyond my baby's differences—let me look with Your eyes, not my own.

Comfort in Times of Trouble

Blessed be the God and Father of our Lord Jesus Christ, the Father of mercies and God of all comfort, who comforts us in all our tribulation, that we may be able to comfort those who are in any trouble, with the comfort with which we ourselves are comforted by God.

—2 Corinthians 1:3–4

Mary's child was born with multiple problems. No one could tell her if Cassie would survive. She could not eat, nor could she breathe easily. Her little face turned blue from the lack of oxygen. Each hour was a struggle. It took hours to squeeze a tiny amount of formula into her.

Five days later, the baby was clinging to life. Mary had been discharged from the hospital, but spent every moment there with Cassie. But that Sunday morning, Mary felt the need to attend church services. She knew the congregation was praying for Cassie; she could see their love and concern in the cards and flowers she and Cassie had received. The church would pray corporately at each of the services for Cassie.

Exhausted and tearful, Mary walked into the church building for the second service of the day. An elderly lady was just leaving the first service. Mary knew a little about her—she was a strong pillar of faith and had raised two handicapped children of her own. When this woman saw Mary, she purposefully made her way across the crowded lobby.

As she reached Mary, she didn't say a word. She simply took Mary's hands and held them. Astonished, Mary saw the woman's eyes fill with tears. Mary was bathed in the warmth and compassion that flowed from this woman. She felt strengthened and understood.

The two women embraced, weeping openly, each understanding the pain of the other. And Mary's heart began to heal.

Returning to the hospital that afternoon, Mary learned that Cassie was stable. Through the next year, many surgeries restored Cassie to good health, although she will always have some disabilities.

But Mary never forgot the healing touch that flowed from God through that elderly woman. Today Mary meets with other mothers of newborns who arrive with problems. She knows that sometimes the best comfort comes from sharing in the other woman's pain, and she gives the same understanding embrace that was given to her that first Sunday morning.

Prayer: Heavenly Father, as You reach out to comfort me, help me to reach out to comfort others. Let me show Your love and compassion wherever it may be needed.

Trust in God

Let not your heart be troubled;
you believe in God, believe also in Me.
—John 14:1

The story is told of a man who stretched a tightrope over the great Niagara Falls. He pranced across it to rousing cheers. Turning, he yelled, "I'm going to do it again!" To the amazement of the crowd, he did! Once more he turned and shouted,

"I'm going to do it again!" which he did. The crowd roared. The man grabbed a wheelbarrow and walked across. The crowd was in a frenzy. He filled the wheelbarrow with dirt and crossed once more. The crowd jumped and shouted.

The man turned to an onlooker and asked, "Do you think I can do it again?" The onlooker replied, "Of course I do!" The man smiled, "So you believe in me?" "Yes!" came the answer, "I believe in you! I do! You are amazing!"

Assured of the man's belief, he dumped out the dirt. Gazing into the onlooker's eyes, he invited, "Climb in."

When our children are born with disabilities or problems, we aren't invited gently into the wheelbarrow; we are thrust in against our wills. We sit, clinging to the edges, whispering desperate prayers. We begin to trust God out of a desperate necessity.

As time passes, we can start to relax our frightened grip, breathe easier, and trust that the wheelbarrow is in the hands of a totally trustworthy God. The tightrope may seem thin and dangerous, but God will never drop us. We can trust Him to continue the journey, though it may be frightening. We can trust Him to steer and to guide, though we may want to steer ourselves. And we can know that no matter the situation, He will not lose His grip.

Loosen your fingers, relax your frightened clinging. Trust the One who steps assuredly on your tightrope. Believe in Him; He will never fail.

Prayer: Lord, help me to trust You even when I am unsure and afraid. Help me to see that the tightrope on which I travel is a smooth, solid path for You.

Songs in the Night

But no one says, "Where is God my Maker,
Who gives songs in the night."
—Job 35:10

I am a trained singer and pianist. I have taught hundreds of young musicians. I have heard Pavarotti, Keith Green, Twila Paris, Mandy Patinkin, and many others. I have seen Baryshnikov dance. I have heard Dizzy Gillespie play. I have seen almost every Tony-award-winning musical that has come to our area. I have seen many of the classical operas. I attend festivals and concerts as often as possible. I study music of other cultures.

I have heard great voices, seen great beauty, and sat awestruck at the hand of God in the breathtaking loveliness of the musical arts. My life has been spent immersed in them as a singer, director, and audience member. God gifted me with a great passion for music, and it is in singing that I feel closest to Him.

Imagine the pain I felt when I was presented with a child of my own who may never speak clearly, let alone sing. I couldn't imagine a life without joyous song pouring forth in worship and praise. How could my son endure that? How could I?

Feeling depressed one evening, I retreated to my basement studio to play my piano and pray. I switched on the baby monitor in order to listen to my sleeping son who rested above me. My fingers touched the keys softly, but no song formed. Tears trickled down my cheeks, and I silently poured my pain before God. My fingers continued traveling lightly across the keys. Gradually a song took shape. I realized, not without surprise, that it was a song of praise. I began to sing, worshiping God without understanding. My heart began to lighten. My voice became loud and full. I sang into the middle of the night, a time of holy communion with the Lord.

Around midnight I suddenly became aware of a noise on the baby monitor, so I stopped. My tears began anew as I realized my little boy was *singing* in his crib. The words were tangled and unclear, but the voice was crystal-pure and strong. It lilted and fell in a beautiful cadence that I recognized as one of the songs of praise I had just finished.

God blessed me that night with the song of my son—a wonderful song of praise in the middle of a dark night. It was a precious gift for my heavy heart.

Prayer: Lord, thank You that even in our darkest night, You will give us songs to comfort, calm, and soothe us. Help us to lift our own songs of praise to You . . . even when we don't understand.

Chosen and Called

And having come in, the angel said to her, "Rejoice, highly favored one, the Lord is with you; blessed are you among women!"

—Luke 1:28

Mary was just a simple Hebrew girl when God called her to the most remarkable of missions: she was to bear a child who would be the Messiah! Mary chose to obey God's call and fulfill His wondrous plan for her life. She could have said no. She could have protected her reputation and safety by turning away. She could have grumbled and complained about God's unsettling her world.

After all, this girl was about to be married to a good Jewish man, a man who was skilled in a worthy trade. She would have lived out her life as a wife and mother, without worrying about things outside her quiet village.

But when she was presented with a unique opportunity to serve God and her people, she chose to say yes, despite the difficulties that would lie ahead of her.

Have you realized yet that you have been chosen and called for a special mission here on this earth?

God has certainly unsettled your world with the birth of your special baby. But in this birth He is giving you the opportunity to serve Him and this little one, despite the difficulties that lie ahead of you.

Your child is not the Messiah. But this baby is an image-bearer of the Lord we serve. God has chosen you—no one else—to raise and to nurture this little one.

You have the choice to go about your mission in obedience or to resent it and complain. You can even turn away from God and His plans for you and your child. But know that His plans are wonderful, even when we don't know what they are.

He has chosen this time out of all eternity to bring you and this little one together. You are called and chosen to a some-times difficult but rewarding mission.

Prayer: Lord, thank You for Your calling upon my life. Help me to fulfill the mission You have set before me. Guide me as I raise this little one for You.

The Thoughtfulness of Others

A harsh word stirs up anger.
—Proverbs 15:1

Sometimes people can say some of the most painful things. When my son was seen for the first time by people outside of the family, he was called a monster and compared to the lead character in *The Hunchback of Notre Dame*. Publications—even *Life* magazine—use the term *harelip* (comparing a cleft-affected child's disability to the split lip of a rabbit) rather than *cleft lip* or *palate*. A famous radio personality recently spoke of something unlovable, comparing it to a "crippled child."

After the first waves of shock wore off, I felt anger in each of these situations. I E-mailed *Life*, called the radio personality, and began to hide my child's face with a blanket.

I was protecting myself from the pain of hearing someone gasp at the sight of my child's deformed face and from the anger that their gasps and thoughtless words stirred within me.

Using that anger to educate others was a positive reaction on my part. Covering my baby, I am ashamed to admit, was not. I just couldn't face someone else who did not see that wonderful boy I held. All that the others saw was his problem, not his chubby cheeks or warm blue eyes.

When Aiden was only five days old, I had already heard enough negative remarks. I needed the solace that only God can provide, so I took my son to a praise gathering at our church. A few women saw him and backed away. I covered his face.

Once in my seat, far from anyone else, I set my sleeping son down in his little car seat. I wept quietly as the music swirled around me.

I became aware that a boy of about fifteen had knelt beside my son. I knew Ben Lenz, having been his director in a musical a few years before. He slowly lowered the blanket covering my baby's face. I held my breath. Gently, Ben brushed his fingertips over Aiden's cheeks and fuzzy round head. Looking up at me, he smiled. "He's beautiful," he whispered.

It was the single most healing moment of my walk with my son. God reached through that teenage boy to touch my heart and give me hope.

Proverbs 15:1 begins with "A soft answer turns away wrath." God used Ben to soothe both my pain and my anger.

Prayer: Lord, help me to channel my anger over thoughtless words into positive results. And help me always to remember the effect my own words may have on others.

Support for the Weak

I have shown you in every way, by laboring like this, that you must support the weak. And remember the words of the Lord Jesus, that He said, "It is more blessed to give than to receive."

—Acts 20:35

Have you ever seen a flock of geese during migration? They fly in magnificent V-patterns that slash across the sky, seeming to stretch from horizon to horizon.

If you look closely, you will notice one goose in the lead, in the point of the V. This leader flaps furiously, acting as a windbreak for the others in the flock until, exhausted, he falls back into the lines of the V. Immediately, another goose flies into the point position and takes over leadership, battling the wind that will soon tire him.

If you have the good fortune to stand outside while one of these mighty flocks soars overhead, you will notice one more thing: the geese in the back are all honking loudly. They are shouting out their own special type of encouragement to the lead goose and to each other.

I'll bet that if we could understand them, we would hear phrases such as, "Keep it up! You're doing great! Almost there! Hang in there!"

The geese are a perfect illustration of the Church. Those who are strong take the lead and, when they need respite and refreshment, they fall back and allow others to lead. The entire group is constantly encouraging others along the way. And they are led by a power they cannot understand, but one that leads them to the correct home with each season.

None of the geese could make the trip alone. They each need the flock to help them with the long journey.

So it is with us. We need a church family to encourage us, lead us, and help us along the way. We cannot make this long journey alone. And we are led by that Power—the Lord— whom we cannot fully understand but who leads us on the correct path toward our home.

Are you weak right now? Fall back and let the flock bring you along. Are you strong? Take your place to help others who may not be. And always follow Him, the One who will lead you with surety and strength.

Prayer: Lord, thank You for the example of the geese. Thank You that you have provided for our care within the community of other believers. Help me to take my proper place in Your flock that I may be strengthened and strengthen others in my turn.

God Sees the Big Picture

For I consider that the sufferings of this present time are not worthy to be compared with the glory which shall be revealed in us.

—Romans 8:18

Faustine took her little girl to a movie theater. The feature was an animated movie with insects as the main characters. As part of the story, the insects were chased by a large, colorful cartoon bird. The bird swept toward the audience until it filled the screen.

With a cry of fright, the little girl threw up her hands to cover her face and fend off the monstrous bird. Faustine stifled a laugh and carefully explained that the bird was not real, and that it certainly was not as large as it seemed.

Her daughter peeked from between her fingers. "See, honey, there is the bird. Now look over there," Faustine said as she pointed to the left. "Now look this way." The little girl turned her head in wonder to see that they were still in the movie theater. She realized that the screen that had overwhelmed her was really a small part of the large room. Emboldened, she turned toward the screen once more. The bird, in its proper perspective, no longer frightened her.

So often we are like this little girl. The problems of raising our special children often seem huge and overwhelming, like the animated bird on the movie screen. But if we take the time to look further at the issues, we can see that there is a bigger picture—one that ultimately falls into God's plan. The problems and struggles become smaller and more manageable in light of all eternity.

We may not see the future. But God does. He knows what is in store for you and your child. And after this life's vapor passes, the bigger picture will finally come into focus for each of us. This present pain will become a distant memory, fading away completely in God's presence.

Hold on to the knowledge of God's bigger picture. There is so much more than today's struggles.

Prayer: Lord, help me to keep in mind the big picture of eternity as I struggle through the daily tasks at hand. Give me Your eternal perspective so that I can truly see what You deem important today.

Taking Matters into Our Own Hands

Now Sarai, Abram's wife, had borne him no children . . . So Sarai said to Abram, "See now, the LORD has restrained me from bearing children. Please, go in to my maid; perhaps I shall obtain children by her."

—Genesis 16:1–2

Sarai wanted a child desperately. Abram had already been promised by God Himself that a son would arrive, but Sarai was impatient. She didn't have God's sense of timing and wisdom, so she decided to take matters into her own hands. Her plan worked . . . in a way. Her maidservant did conceive a son, but the consequences for Sarai and her family were dire. Not only did the maidservant despise her mistress, but the son and his descendants have been in conflict with Israel throughout history.

Eventually, in God's perfect time, Sarai did conceive a son who was the heir to God's promises to Abram. Had Sarai waited with patience, all that God had promised would have come to pass without the added complication of Sarai's actions . . . and consequences.

Lucille had given birth to a child with severe problems. She knew that those problems could be surgically corrected, but she was desperate for a miraculous healing. She prayed fervently for divine intervention. She marshaled others to pray with her.

But God's plan and time were different from that which Lucille demanded of Him. He answered her prayer with His own request to wait upon Him and trust that His plan was best.

Impatient, Lucille began to search for her own path. One afternoon as she traveled with her child, she saw a flashing sign that read "Miracles! Healing! No one turned away!" She pulled into the driveway with anticipation.

But as she stepped from the car, she felt an unsettling in her spirit. She saw strange symbols and pictures of animal sacrifice through the windows. She knew without a doubt that she should get back in the car and flee, but she kept moving forward.

Once inside the doors she was immediately surrounded by people in flowing white robes. They snatched her baby from her and began dancing around the room. In a panic, she grabbed the child back but found she couldn't reach the door. She made her escape by paying a substantial "fee" for their prayers and "healing" touch. Once in the car, she cried out to God for forgiveness. She had doubted Him and tried to go her own way. Eventually through surgery and God's able hand, her baby was restored to a mostly "normal" appearance. And Lucille carries with her the knowledge that God's plan is best—and we can run into real danger when we try to insert our own plans into His.

Prayer: Lord, forgive us for not trusting You when we try to solve our troubles in our own ways. Help us to trust in Your timing and Your perfect plan for our lives.

The Destructive Power of Jealousy

And from that time on Saul kept a jealous eye on David.
—1 Samuel 18:9 NIV

Saul was anointed by God to lead Israel, but his jealousy of David became his ultimate undoing. What started as ill feeling grew into a murder attempt and eventually to a destructive war. Jealousy may start small, but it can grow to disastrous proportions.

Sherry gave birth to her third child, a son, only to find out he had a severe case of Down's syndrome. Her little one lived only two days. She never even got to hold him.

For years, Sherry grieved the loss of her boy. She began cutting off ties with friends who were starting their own families.

She couldn't bear to see their healthy babies. She began to despise the women who were happily raising them.

Five years later her sister, Kathy, met a wonderful man who had been through his own private pain over losing contact with a rebellious daughter years earlier. When Kathy and Mike married, both extended families rejoiced in the new beginning for them.

They were ecstatic when, five months later, Kathy announced that she was pregnant. All of them, that is, except Sherry. She began avoiding her sister.

In the eighth month of pregnancy, Kathy suddenly had a searing headache. Mike rushed her to the hospital where she was immediately placed on a helicopter and flown to a hospital in a larger city. Mike almost lost both his wife and his son that day. But God mercifully intervened, and both of them survived eclampsia, a very dangerous condition.

After weeks in the hospital the little family was reunited at home. Well-wishers gathered and brought gifts. The baby grew and thrived and became a joyful member of the clan. But Sherry wouldn't visit. She wouldn't hold the baby. She began to despise her sister who, even though she experienced a near-fatal illness, had a healthy baby.

And now Sherry is isolated, by her own choice, from the joys of watching her nephew grow. Kathy continues to try to bridge the gap between them, but Sherry's jealousy overrides all other emotions and desires.

The death of her son has become an ever-increasing tragedy.

Prayer: Lord, when I am tempted to be jealous at the sight of a healthy and whole baby, help me to remember that this child's wholeness has nothing to do with my child's problems. Enable me to rejoice with new mothers in the miracle of Your creation.

We, Too, Can Be a Refuge

In the fear of the LORD there is strong confidence,
And His children will have a place of refuge.
—Proverbs 14:26

As we rely on God, learning to respect and trust Him, He becomes our fortress of protection against this fallen world and its pain. He keeps us in peace and strengthens us for our daily walk. And as our faith grows, we become a help to our children.

A wise woman once told me that it is best to take our children out into the public eye in order to expose them to people's reactions to their disabilities. My first instinct was to argue with her—I wanted to protect my child from stares and hurtful (no matter how unintended) comments. I wanted to keep him safe in my home with those who loved him.

"But what better time to allow our children to experience these hurts—when they can turn to us for comfort and support?" she gently questioned.

She was right. Our children will be hurt at some point by someone who may not understand their differences. We have the unique opportunity to instruct our children during these times. We can explain the situation, whether it is caused by ignorance or cruelty, and help our child brainstorm ideas to handle it. In the process we stand as signposts for our children, pointing them toward the One who can help the hurt and give them value and worth.

And when our child has processed the situation and moved on (they can be very resilient!), we in turn can enter the fortress He provides. When our child hurts, we hurt even more. God provides the same fortress of protection for our hearts that He gives our children.

Our children will witness firsthand that turning to God is the solution for anything life may throw at us. They will come to trust that the Fortress sheltering Mommy is a trustworthy refuge for their souls.

There is no better protection we can offer our children.

Prayer: You are a mighty fortress, a refuge for me and my child. Thank You for the protection You offer each of us.

Assigned

> LORD, you have assigned me my portion and my cup.
> —Psalm 16:5 NIV

Most of us have had our share of assignments. Growing up, we were assigned chores at home. We had assignments in school. We may have attended college or job training before landing a job—which itself is a series of assigned tasks. Now we have been assigned roles in our homes, in our relationships, and in virtually every aspect of life. We also have been assigned positions in ministry: to our immediate family, our church, our world.

Have you thought about the unique assignment given by God in the raising of your special child? It is no accident that you have this child. This baby has been assigned to you; your child with differences is your portion and cup.

Just as Jesus prayed to have the cup removed from Him in Gethsemane, there may be times we pray for the load to lessen. God never promised that our cup would be any easier than the one Jesus drank.

The promise to believers is not that God will make our lives easier. He simply promises to make our lives eternal. While we live on earth, our days may be hard. But He did promise to be there to help us carry the load.

Our cup may be less full than others. It may be dry and bitter, or it may be sweet and refreshing. At times it may be both. The cup itself may be chipped and cracked, but it is exactly the cup we have been handed by a compassionate and loving God.

We drink of it, relying on Him to sweeten it in His time.

Our assignment is to take our portion and live our lives to glorify Him, whether or not we wanted this particular cup.

Prayer: Lord, I accept the cup You have assigned me. Help me to fulfill my assignment for Your glory and the benefit of my child.

God Is the Strength for the Weak

My flesh and my heart fail;
But God is the strength of my heart and my portion forever.
                                             —Psalm 73:26

Mary was a cross-country runner. She had been an active participant in competition throughout high school and college, winning state championships and national honors. During one grueling meet, she finished the final mile of the run on an uphill stretch. Exhausted, she crossed the finish line and collapsed forward, utterly spent. Just as she was about to hit the ground, strong hands raised her up. The man who had been the starter, firing the pistol to send the runners off, had placed himself at the finish line to help the exhausted runners at the completion of their race. His compassionate aid kept Mary from falling as he helped her limp around the course until her own strength returned.

Mary was forever grateful for the kindness of that man. They developed a friendship that lasted until the end of his life. She continues a friendship with his wife to this day.

Are you running a long, hard race? Is exhaustion defeating you? Look ahead, runner, to the finish line. The Starter of your race is awaiting you at the finish. But, unlike Mary's friend, He is also running beside you, encouraging you to continue, lifting you in His arms, and giving you strength. Let Him help you limp along until your own strength returns.

Your strength may fail you from time to time. But God's strength never fails. He is awaiting the chance to raise you up and help you. He will give you the strength and the rest you so desperately desire.

Each step of the race, each day, each hour depends on this loving help. Don't try to do it alone in your own weakness. Our own strength is nothing compared to the One who is all-powerful. Fall into His arms today, surrender your race to Him, and watch where He will take you.

Prayer: Lord, I surrender my weakness to You. I rely on Your strength, Your compassion, and Your love to get me through today. I know You are with me, helping me limp along whenever my strength fails.

A Good Word ❋

Being confident of this very thing, that He who has begun a good work in you will complete it until the day of Jesus Christ.
—Philippians 1:6

Bernadette is an artist. She has an eye for beauty and a gift for transferring that beauty into tangible objects. She has carved intricately detailed wooden statues, drawn lifelike sketches of children and animals, and transformed her home into a virtual museum. But her standout gift is in oil painting.

Bernadette has painted several works, all of which are breathtaking. An artist signs a work when it is completed, but Bernadette has never signed any of hers. She has never yet been satisfied with her paintings. She might put one aside for a time only to return to it, slightly altering a color or the shading. When others tell her that the painting is wonderful . . . perfect . . . ready to hang, Bernadette smiles and tells them that the artist's eyes still see areas that need work. And with each minor touch, the painting becomes even more beautiful than before.

When Bernadette's son, Jacob, was born with a heart defect, her world was turned upside down. She abandoned her studio to spend her time at Jacob's side in the pediatric unit of a large hospital. Doctors worked frantically to bring his condition under control. Slowly Jacob's blue skin began to turn pink. Medicine dosages were adjusted, and his condition became less dire.

Eventually, Jacob went home with a monitor and medications that will keep him alive. Over time, Bernadette adjusted to her changed life.

When she is asked about Jacob, she smiles and tells others that he is a work in progress. She sees that the Artist responsible is still at work, adjusting and retouching the creation that is her son. Each time she looks at him, she sees that he is even more beautiful than before.

Bernadette knows that Jacob is God's artistic masterpiece, and with each adjustment this good work grows ever closer to completion. "But the signature will be placed when Jacob meets the Lord face-to-face—when he is complete and whole—in heaven."

Prayer: Lord, You are the artist at work in the life of my child. You adjust and change and move this little one ever closer to the completion of Your own good work. Thank You that I am witness to the process. I look forward to the time when You will place Your signature on this completed work of art . . . this beautiful, precious child.

Choose Joy

And let your heart cheer you in the days of your youth.
—Ecclesiastes 11:9

We have a choice in how we live each day. We can live it in defeat and depression, or we can live it in victory and joy.

Choose joy!

Life has its hardships and pain. But each day has its moments of joy that can lift us above the mundane and difficult moments. Spend your day looking for those wonderful little blessings God sends to lighten our hearts.

When you change a diaper, tickle a tummy. When you wash a face, play peek-a-boo. When you bathe a child, breathe in the incredible smell of freshly lotioned baby skin. As you travel to the doctor, sing in the car . . . make up silly songs using your child's name . . . sing praises for the day you share with your child. Hold your little one close and rock him as he sleeps.

Choose joy!

Look for the funny moments even in the midst of the disasters. One couple had spent a difficult evening with their children. The older kids were jealous of the time spent with the youngest, who was disabled. They voiced their displeasure with arguments and back talk. The baby screamed for an hour while the mother walked back and forth with him in her arms. The father bathed the others and dressed them in pajamas. After struggling to get the children into bed, a process that seemed to take hours that night, the exhausted parents slumped onto the couch to watch the weather forecast. Just as the announcer appeared, the television set made a "poof" sound and went black. The couple looked at the blank television and then at each other. And they began to laugh—it seemed to them to be the perfect finale for a chaotic day!

There are moments of joy everywhere. Is the sun shining? Is

a gentle rain wetting the lawn? Are birds singing? Is the snow sparkling? Look to the wonder of nature to see God's hand.

Look at your wonderful baby. Does he have soft skin? Is there fuzzy hair on a round head? Are there sparkling eyes? Is there a tiny nose? Fingers? Toes? For whatever may be missing, there are surely many other beautiful features on that little one's body.

Don't live in defeat. Choose joy!

Prayer: Lord, just for today, I am going to find two things to be joyful in for every difficult circumstance. Just for today, I choose joy!

Fix Your Eyes on Jesus

> *And let us run with endurance the race that is set before us, looking unto Jesus, the author and finisher of our faith.*
>
> —Hebrews 12:1–2

One warm summer day the world was shocked by a plane crash off the coast of Martha's Vineyard. Three promising lives were lost when a plane piloted by John F. Kennedy Jr. crashed into the ocean.

Theories about the cause of the crash were immediately discussed, taking into account the darkness at the time of the crash, hazy conditions, and the young man's lack of training in flying exclusively with the plane's instruments.

One theory contends that Kennedy may have become disoriented by the lack of any type of visual landmark. The sky looked exactly like the ocean. Everything was black. The pilot may have lost his bearings and tried to right the plane, only to end up spinning out of control into the black waves.

These three people may have been lost because Kennedy had nothing on which to fix his eyes.

We, too, can lose our bearings when we lose sight of our landmark—Jesus. Paul exhorts us to keep our eyes fixed on Him so that we may complete the race marked out for us. Without Jesus to follow, we may lose our bearings, try to "right" our lives according to our instincts or the advice of others, and end up spinning out of control into the black waters of despair, anger, and confusion.

Jesus will keep us on course even in the darkest of nights, when our sight is too hazy to trust. He will guide us with His Spirit if only we keep our eyes on Him.

So run with perseverance, stick to the course, stay fixed on Jesus.

Prayer: Lord, keep my eyes on You. Help me to endure, lead me safely over the course of the race, and bring me to the finish line in Your time.

Endure for the Joy Set Before You

Who for the joy that was set before Him endured the cross.
—Hebrews 12:2

The greatest example of endurance we can look to is Jesus Himself. He lived a life on this earth that was filled with pain and hardship, sorrow and compassion. Not only did He grieve the rejection He saw in the lives of His chosen people, He endured torture and a terrible death.

But during His thirty-plus years on earth Jesus willingly walked the path marked out before Him because He knew that the temporary pain here was simply a prelude to the eternal joy set before Him.

His pain and death gained so much for so many. Because of it, we can be called children of God and receive the gifts of forgiveness and eternal life. We rejoice in the sacrifice Jesus made on our behalf . . . even as we grieve the fact that it caused Him pain.

In a reflection of that most perfect example, our walk on earth is also filled with trials and pain. Our special children may endure hardship because of their differences. But this temporary pain can be used to bring us into the joy that is set before us in Christ.

Perhaps the problems our children face are the reason we are seeking God today. Maybe God will use our children to nudge other people into a closer relationship with Him. Some may begin searching for answers and come to the one Truth.

I can think of no greater honor than to know that, because of my child, other people have come to know Christ, and in so doing, will enter into heaven one day. My son has been the catalyst for their having a closer walk with God. He has been that same catalyst in my own life.

This present pain can indeed be the prelude to eternal joy.

Prayer: Lord, use the pain of this life to bring both me and my child into a closer relationship with You. Thank You that this pain is temporary but Your joy is eternal.

Calming the Storm   ❧

Then they cry out to the LORD in their trouble . . .
He calms the storm,
So that its waves are still.
                              —Psalm 107:28–29

All of her life Colleen had a fear of storms. The sudden, sizzling flashes of light, the roar of the wind, and the explosions of thunder would send her running from room to room with her hands clamped firmly over her ears. She would try to escape the fear by constant movement, movement that would continue until the storm faded.

When her child was born with multiple problems, Colleen was thrown into another type of storm. Her life became a series of struggles that threatened to overwhelm her.

True to the learned behavior of her childhood, Colleen dealt with her fear by staying in constant motion. By never allowing herself time to be still, she avoided dealing with her complex feelings over her daughter.

If she stayed busy cleaning, researching, calling, working with her daughter, and myriad other tasks, her days were full, and her grief and fear were held at bay.

Seeing her friend at the point of exhaustion, a wise woman took Colleen aside. "You must take the time to experience your feelings. You have become a 'human doing,' rather than a 'human being.' Take the time to just *be*."

But when Colleen slowed, she could see the lightning and hear the wind and thunder of her life. Trembling in fear, she was on the brink of a serious breakdown.

Her wise friend once again intervened. "Have you asked the Lord to calm this storm?"

As though struck by the lightning she so feared, Colleen answered that she had not. The two friends immediately knelt in prayer, crying out to God.

"Almost immediately I felt a new kind of peace and strength. My life is still complicated, my daughter's problems have not faded—that is all still there. But the calm . . . the quiet . . . was created inside me," Colleen now says with a smile.

Colleen doesn't feel the compulsion anymore to fill every moment with activity. She takes the time to feel—whether the emotions are painful or happy. And she stays in close touch with the God who calmed her storm.

Prayer: Lord, in the midst of the storm, You are a calming force. Help me to seek shelter in Your safe harbor until the storms fade.

Look Forward

And God will wipe away every tear from their eyes; there shall be no more death, nor sorrow, nor crying. There shall be no more pain, for the former things have passed away.

—Revelation 21:4

Look forward, dear mother, to the day when your child is perfectly whole. See the future the Lord holds for you and your little one, when one day you will dwell together with Him in heaven.

He promises that the pain will end. Nor will you continue to weep over your child—there will be no reason for tears! You'll mourn your losses no longer, for all will be restored.

One day you will enter into His presence, and He will gently call your name. When you approach, the Lord Himself will raise a gentle hand to your face to wipe away all the years of crying. He will take you into His arms and whisper that your struggles are over. He will tell you that you have completed the race and can now rest with Him. You will look into those eyes filled with love and compassion, and you will know that He has been there for every moment of anguish, every difficult day.

He has laughed with you in joy and wept with you in sorrow. He has loved your child with a perfect love . . . a love that encompasses you too. He has reached out to enfold both of you in the circle of His protection. He has lifted you with His strength on those days when you felt you simply could not go on.

And through it all, He has been making a place for you. A safe place where the struggle will never again bring you to your knees in pain. A place where you and your child will forget the short time you toiled on earth. A place where each day is filled with the joyous presence of Jesus. A place that is your rightful home.

Prayer: Lord, one day my child and I will enter into that place where pain and struggle are no more. Help me to keep my eyes focused on that hope, which is mine through a saving relationship with You.

He's Preparing a Place for You

I go to prepare a place for you. And if I go and prepare a place for you, I will come again and receive you to Myself; that where I am, there you may be also.

—John 14:2–3

When Jerrie's baby was born with spina bifida, the family realized that several modifications would have to be made to their house. The first-floor bedroom would have to be converted for Rachel's use. Special equipment would have to be purchased. The front porch would have to be removed and a wheelchair ramp installed. Counters in the kitchen would have to be lowered for Rachel's convenience. Their family car would eventually be replaced by a van with a wheelchair lift.

Lovingly, Jerrie and her husband made painstaking improvements to their home and yard, giving Rachel full access to every place on the property. Soon paved paths snaked through the garden so that Rachel could enjoy the fragrance of roses. Apple trees were pruned and bent so that Rachel could smell the blossoms in the spring and pick the fruit in the fall. A cement chute entered the pond, allowing Rachel to move her chair into the water on hot summer days.

Jerrie worked for years to make Rachel's home a welcome and useful place.

Just as Jerrie prepared her home for Rachel, Jesus is preparing an eternal home for her, a truth Rachel learned one morning in Sunday school.

Bursting with excitement, Rachel told her mother how Jesus was making a special home for her in heaven. Jerrie turned pained eyes on her daughter, ready to explain that Jesus would not have to make a "special" house for Rachel, like the one she currently inhabited. But before she could speak, Rachel continued.

"And this place, my place in heaven, won't have special paths or short counters or wheelchair ramps or anything else like that. And do you know why?"

Jerrie shook her head as tears filled her eyes.

"Because I will be perfect! Jesus said so in the Bible!"

Amen.

Prayer: Lord, thank You that You prepare a special place for our little ones . . . and for us. Thank You that heaven will have no wheelchair ramps, no special equipment, no needles, no hospitals, and no pain. We look forward to the day You return to take us there to dwell with You forever.

It Has Been Overcome

In the world you will have tribulation; but be of good cheer, I have overcome the world.

—John 16:33

The dictionary on my desk says that *to overcome* means "to overpower" or "prevail over."

This reminds me of the wrestling meets I watched throughout my lifetime. My father was a high school coach, and both of my brothers wrestled at the state level of competition. One even qualified for national competition in college.

They rose to that level of proficiency through dedication, perseverance, and practice. After years of preparation, my brothers could walk confidently onto the mat for the match.

Oftentimes their opponent was also well prepared for battle. My brothers would use every move they had learned, every instinct with which they had been gifted, and every careful plan they had prepared. Finally, they would hear the resounding slap of the official's hand on the mat, signaling their victory. But sometimes that same slap and whistle would signify their defeat.

After a victory, they would celebrate and begin training once again for the next battle. After a defeat, they would analyze what had gone wrong and strategize plans to prevent it from occurring again. I remember sitting for hours watching my father help my brothers become the best wrestlers they could be, able to overcome their adversaries.

And so it is for us in our life as believers. We face battles in this life, many of which have a spiritual, rather than physical, root.

Your child's differences may be physical, but the real battle is underneath where evil tries to take root in our soul by planting seeds of bitterness and despair.

We go "onto the mat" every day. When we are well prepared through a strong reliance on the Lord and His Word, we come out victorious. But when we take our eyes away from God and forget His path, we can be defeated.

After each victory, we can celebrate and resume our "training" to prepare for future battles. After a loss, we can analyze what went wrong and turn to our Father, who will help us to become the best Christians we can be, able to overcome the adversary through His strength.

Prayer: Lord, as I step into the battle today, help me to overcome what You have already defeated. Help me to use my training and relationship with You to win today's battles.

Time with God   ❧

Joshua said to the children of Israel, "Come here, and hear the words of the LORD your God."

—Joshua 3:9

Joshua and the Israelites had a big day ahead of them. They had consecrated themselves and made final preparations for their entrance into the promised land. They had wandered for forty years in the desert before this day could occur.

But in the midst of the preparation and busyness, Joshua called the people aside to listen to the Word of God. They purposefully chose to spend time listening to God before they broke camp and proceeded with their day.

It can be so difficult to find time to spend with God when the demands of our special children consume our day. The fact that you are reading this shows your desire to seek His Word. God is blessed when you spend this time with Him. And so are you.

There are many ways in which to keep time with God from slipping out of your busy life.

- Purchase or make Scripture verse cards. Place them on a shelf or windowsill above your kitchen sink. At each mealtime, prop a card before you and meditate on that verse.
- Purchase or borrow the Bible on tape. Turn on the tape when you feed your baby. Let the Word of God fill your home and your heart.
- Arrange with your spouse or a friend to watch the children for two hours once a week so that you may attend a Bible study.
- Invite a friend to your home for a one-on-one Bible study once a week during nap time.
- Set your alarm fifteen minutes early and spend that time in the Bible.
- Find a prayer partner with whom you will share a short phone call each day to pray and share a Bible verse.

The Lord will honor the time you spend seeking Him—no matter how short that time may be. As your routine becomes easier or more familiar, you may be able to extend the time you spend in concentrated quiet time with the Lord.

But for now, don't feel guilty about the snatches of time you grab to be with Him. He judges the desire and quality, not just the quantity of time.

Prayer: Lord, thank You for the times that I am able to spend with You in Your Word. Help me to find ways to increase that time of renewal and relationship.

Put on the Armor

Put on the whole armor of God, that you may be able to stand against the wiles of the devil.

—Ephesians 6:11

I recently directed the musical *Camelot,* which is based on the King Arthur legend. In the play, several of the characters, knights of the round table, take part in a joust, a scene that required special costuming to represent armor. Our costumer fashioned beautiful metal plates and cloth into these suits of armor.

The result was breathtaking . . . in more ways than one. The costumes were beautiful but heavy and durable, a characteristic for which we were grateful during the last week of rehearsals.

Danny, one of the knights, was wearing his armor and waiting for his entrance. With a sudden crack, one of the set pieces broke free and swung toward him. A jagged board hit Danny full in the chest, knocking him backward. We rushed to help him to his feet. He was fine, but the wind had been knocked out of him, and there was a huge dent in his metal breastplate. Wearing the fake armor had actually protected him from what could have been disastrous.

How much more are we protected from disaster when we consciously don the armor of God that Paul described in Ephesians 6: the belt of truth, the breastplate of righteousness, the shoes of preparation of the gospel of peace, the shield of faith, the helmet of salvation, and the sword of the Spirit.

Have you noticed that every piece of armor described here except one is for defense, not aggression or offense? The armor is for protection. The sword alone, the Word of God, is the one weapon with which to reach out and slay our enemy.

We enter a battlefield each day as we raise our special children in this imperfect world. Satan eagerly seeks our weakest, most vulnerable moments to launch his vicious attacks. He may whisper accusations about our part in our children's differences. He may bring to light further problems, weaving a mood of despair around us. Though we may not be sure of which form the attacks may take, we can certainly be sure they will come.

As you battle with Satan for control of your moment-by-moment existence, protect yourself with God's armor. It will keep you safe from the devil's attacks. And then allow God to defeat the devil with His Word. Stand ready against the devil's schemes of despair and anger and complacency.

Start your day by actually talking yourself through the process of donning your armor. "I am claiming the belt of truth. I am wearing the breastplate of righteousness. My feet are fitted with the preparation of the gospel. I carry the shield of faith. I don the helmet of salvation. I carry the sword of the Spirit. I have all of these things through the Lord, who promises to keep me safe in today's battle."

Prayer: (Read aloud the paragraph above . . . and continue your day ready for battle!)

The Belt of Truth   ❧

Stand therefore, having girded your waist with truth . . .
—Ephesians 6:14

As an ancient soldier prepared his armor, he donned his belt, both as protection and a functional part of his attire. A belt is meant for support. It completes the entire outfit, holding everything else together, giving support to our most vulnerable areas. The belt would be used to hold the warrior's sword at the ready. Hence, the belt, a seemingly unimportant part of the garment, was actually a foundational part of daily preparations.

Such is the case with truth in our lives. Jesus claimed to be the truth (John 14:6). There is nothing of Him that is false. His words are truth. His salvation is truth. His gospel is truth. His love is truth. His compassion is truth.

His love for you and your child is truth.

God's truth is real. It wraps around you both like the belt of a garment. It holds you together and completes you. It keeps your vulnerable and private parts—your thoughts and your emotions—covered and safe. It can be worn in confidence for any to see and realize that your God is your truth. It is the assurance against failure, and sin, and is a foundational part of our daily preparations.

God's truth is written out for you in the Bible. It is available to you whenever you reach out for it. You can read it at will or memorize a verse to be recalled when needed. It can be your daily strength and encouragement, calming your spirit and helping you through each moment of your day as you raise your special child.

As you prepare for this day, take a moment to don the belt of truth. Spend a moment in prayer, read a verse from God's Word. Write it on an index card or slip of paper and carry it with you today. Pull it out periodically and read it over. Commit it to memory and write it on your heart.

Gird yourself with this belt of protection and completion.

Prayer: Lord, today I wear Your truth around me. Wrapped in its safety, I begin this day. Bring Your Word to my mind throughout the day. Thank You for Jesus, the truth You share with me today.

The Breastplate of Righteousness

> . . . *having put on the breastplate of righteousness.*
> —Ephesians 6:14

Righteousness can be described as the state of being morally right, honest, proper, and just. God's righteousness is a holiness that sets us apart, giving us a guiltlessness that shows we have been forgiven of our sins. We are made righteous through the sacrifice of Jesus. At the moment we receive the gift of His death and eternal life, we are set apart—made holy—by God.

It can be a struggle for us to accept this definition when it is applied to us. Each day we fail by losing our patience, by complaining, by sinning in a multitude of ways. But when we lay our failings before God, He once again forgives us and makes us pure.

We do not carry our guilt and sin with us. God cleanses us and makes us His, removing our sin and making us whole.

This protection of righteousness is described as a breastplate. In ancient times, the breastplate was worn to protect that most vital of human organs—the heart. God's righteousness protects our heart from the attacks of the evil one.

Is your heart broken over the differences in your child? God is there to protect your aching heart from becoming hard and bitter, turning to sin.

Is your heart failing with exhaustion? God is there to protect your heart from complaining and losing patience.

Is your heart angry and disillusioned? God is there to protect your heart from giving up, and He can fill it with hope.

Is your heart filled with guilt over your child's condition? God is there to wash away that guilt and make you clean . . . whether that guilt is merited or not.

Is your heart vulnerable because of the strife in your life? God is there to guard it from the silent attacks of the enemy.

Rest in the knowledge that your fragile heart has the best protection there is: the breastplate of righteousness, fashioned for you by the holy, righteous God.

Prayer: Lord, thank You for the protection You give my heart. Today I claim the breastplate of righteousness You have given me to cover my heart and keep it safe from anything that would turn it from You.

Shod with Readiness

. . . and having shod your feet with
the preparation of the gospel of peace.
—Ephesians 6:15

Many of us have walked barefoot outside. The grass and dirt beneath our feet may be soft and welcoming. It may be pleasant to step through the dew-soaked lawn early in the day. In the same way, the warmth of a dirt path may bring pleasurable sensations.

But what happens when, during our barefoot walk, we encounter burrs or gravel or hot pavement? We cringe and try to find a way around the obstruction, only to have to travel painfully through it in many situations. Oftentimes we must turn back and put shoes on our feet before traversing that particular path with success.

Have you hit gravel or hot pavement in your walk? Have you sought ways around these things? Are you resigned to travel painfully through this difficult time?

Stop and put on your shoes. Fit your feet with readiness—the type of readiness that will allow you to face any situation with the peace of God that comes only through His truth. Build a relationship with the Lord that will sustain you and protect your feet so that you will not slip on this difficult path before you.

Raising a child with differences is not easy. There will be moments of great joy and celebration, but there will also be moments of great pain and sorrow. It is for those moments that God has prepared those special shoes.

Not only has He prepared them, He lovingly puts them in place on your feet when you step forward to wear them, having spent time in preparation: reading the Bible, praying, and learning to walk with God. God will also walk with you to be sure the shoes do their proper job!

During World War II, army forces placed stakes in the ground to wound the feet of the opposing soldiers. They knew that if the feet were compromised, the soldier would be taken out of the battle.

Our enemy knows that this is true even in spiritual battle. If your feet are not ready to travel, to stay on the path before you, and to stand firm when your faith is challenged, you could lose the battle.

But the Lord is protecting those feet—and your faith—during your travels in this life. And as you walk, no matter where you walk, He will help you in this journey with His strength and peace.

Prayer: Lord, fit my feet with Your readiness. Fill me with Your peace.

The Shield of Faith

. . . above all, taking the shield of faith with which you will be able to quench all the fiery darts of the wicked one.

—Ephesians 6:16

Is your faith wavering, dear mother? That can happen from time to time as you come to terms with your child's problems.

But remember that when your faith wavers, God is waiting to strengthen it. All you need to do is ask Him.

The Bible tells us that anyone lacking faith need only ask, and God will supply it. So faith is a gift from Him, not something we have to manufacture on our own. We just ask for it and then receive it from His loving hand.

The faith He gives is our shield. We can use it to fend off the fiery darts that will be sent our way.

Picture an ancient battle. God's people are defending their strongholds. Flaming arrows are sent in volley after volley toward them. Their shields are not the little ones worn on the forearm like those of medieval times. These shields are large enough for a person to crouch behind. They protect the entire body. The arrows simply hit the shield and bounce off, falling uselessly to the ground.

This is the type of shield God provides for you. It is large enough for you to hide completely behind. Every part of you is protected and hidden from the onslaught meant to destroy you. As each flaming arrow arrives, picture it bouncing off your shield, falling smoldering to the ground.

Has today been difficult? Did you find arrow after arrow coming your way, threatening your safety, your solace, and your faith? Is your relationship with God at risk because of the onslaught? Are the flaming arrows of doubt, anger, sorrow, or despair flying your way? Duck behind the shield of faith. Let God protect you in the battle today.

You need only ask.

Prayer: Lord, thank You for providing the shield of faith behind which I can hide. Give me the full measure of faith when mine wavers. Help me to remain steadfast in You.

The Helmet of Salvation

And take the helmet of salvation.
—Ephesians 6:17

Salvation is the greatest gift God offers. While we were still living in our sin, lost and estranged from God, Jesus came to us and took our sins upon Himself. He voluntarily walked to His own execution, knowing that by doing so He fulfilled the blood sacrifice on our behalf.

This gift stands before each one of us, ready for the taking. We don't have to be "good enough" or go through several difficult tasks to earn it. We certainly don't deserve it, being sinful people.

But God loves you so much that He was willing to suffer a terrible death to gift you with His salvation.

Have you received the gift yet? If not, take a moment to read the Afterword of this book. If you have received the gift, but have drifted away, take this time to renew your commitment to God. Ask His forgiveness, and invite Him into the rightful place in your life today.

Take the helmet of salvation and allow God to place it on your head, protecting your mind. And when doubts or evil thoughts creep in, claim the power of that helmet over your mind. Allow the Holy Spirit of God to control your thoughts and keep them pure and grounded in Him.

Seize the protective head covering offered you today. Not only will God protect your mind, He will give you the strength to continue in this struggle we face each day. Work each day to concentrate on renewing your mind by reading a verse from the Bible and committing it to memory.

Reach out and grasp this helmet with both hands, taking possession of the gift of salvation offered to you. Take hold of it as though your life depended on that helmet.

Because it does.

Prayer: Lord, it is unfathomable that You love me so much that You would suffer and die on my behalf. Thank You for this awesome gift. Place the helmet firmly on my head as a protection for not only my mind, but my eternity.

The Sword of the Spirit

And the sword of the Spirit, which is the word of God.
—Ephesians 6:17

The one weapon we have in our spiritual armor is the sword. A sword can divide, cut, or thrust. It can be used to parry the advances of the enemy.

The best warriors in ancient times were those skilled at swordplay. When the battle commenced and the early volleys of arrows and other thrown objects were spent, the hand-to-hand combat determined the winner of the fight. There was little occasion to rely on the aid of others who were engaged in their own battles. It was simply one warrior against another, both armed with weapons meant for close contact. The soldier had to depend on the fact that his sword was strong, able to take blows, and that he had enough skill to use it well.

In today's battles against the realm of evil, we, too, move in for conflicts that are close to us. The enemy may enter with his lies about you or your child or your God. It is then that you can parry his sword thrust with the sword of the Spirit, the Word of God. For every lie the enemy aims at you, God's Word will destroy it.

Your sword is made of indestructible material. It is tempered and sharp. With it you can thrust, cut, parry, and divide. With it you can destroy the enemy's attacks. Satan cannot stand against the Word of God.

Arm yourself. Read the Bible. Study it in a small group, or a one-on-one Bible study. Listen to the Bible on tape. Memorize Scripture verses to use when the attacks come. Attend a church where the Word of God is strongly preached. Find a godly woman to mentor you. Listen to Christian radio and CDs. In as many ways as possible, fill your mind with the Word of God.

And then, when the battle is heated and close, you will have a weapon with a power beyond all others with which to defend yourself.

Prayer: Lord, I take up the challenge. I know that the enemy will come against me as I seek to draw closer to You. He will make accusations and whisper his lies, hoping to draw me off course. Fill my mind with Your Word so that I carry the sword of the Spirit with me each day, ever ready to win the battle.

But It Is My Fault

If we confess our sins, He is faithful and just to forgive us our sins and to cleanse us from all unrighteousness.

—1 John 1:9

How painful it is to carry the burden of knowing that your actions may have been the cause of your child's problems. Even if the actions preceding the problem were not intentional, the grief and sorrow and guilt are still there. How much more so when the actions taken were deliberate and possibly sinful.

Take heart, dear mother. There is forgiveness awaiting the chance to lift that burden and purify you. God needs only for you to confess it to Him and ask for forgiveness . . . and forgiveness will be yours. It is a promise God Himself makes to you.

He longs for you to crawl into His lap and whisper your pain. He invites you to tell Him what it is you may have done. He calls you to confess it to Him. He desires to give you the forgiveness He offers.

This promise holds. Once you confess to Him and receive His forgiveness, the sin is gone, nevermore to be remembered by Him. He will remove it from you as far as the east is from the west (Ps. 103:12). He will see you as clean and whole.

Now, we must remember that this promise does not mean that He will always remove the consequences resulting from our actions. Your child may always bear the problems that were the result of a specific action. It is the same as a criminal who ends up in jail. God will forgive a repentant criminal, but He may not remove Him from the prison.

Granted, the Lord can provide a miracle at any time. But His will may be a different plan for us.

The challenge for us, then, once God has forgiven us, is to forgive ourselves. Scripture calls us to forgive one another. That seems so much easier than forgiving ourselves. But Scripture says that if there is "one" among you who has sinned and is repentant, we are to forgive. Are you not "one"?

Speak your forgiveness aloud. Right now say "Just as the Lord has forgiven me, I forgive myself." Any time you slip into guilt or self-contempt, repeat this message of forgiveness aloud.

Your child will be blessed by the peace that forgiveness will bring you. And remember, your child's problems are not eternal! And God may be using these temporary problems to bring you, your child, and others to Himself.

Prayer: Lord, I ask Your forgiveness for my actions and unbelief. Just as You forgive me, I forgive myself. Thank You for this new beginning.

God Can Make Good Out of Anything

> *And we know that all things work together for good to those who love God, to those who are the called according to His purpose.*
> —Romans 8:28

God's intention at the beginning of time was never that of causing pain to His people. But with the fall of man and the entrance of sin into the picture, so came pain and suffering.

Sometimes God authors that pain in order to draw us away from a destructive lifestyle that could cost us for eternity. At times, He may allow pain in order to motivate us to reach out to others. Perhaps, some of the struggles we face are His way of molding us into the vessels into which and through which He can pour innumerable blessings.

It isn't easy to accept these explanations when the person affected is our child. It would be so much easier to accept the pain or affliction into our own bodies, rather than those of our children. But God has another path for us to follow.

Sometimes the problems our children have are specifically authored by Satan in order to turn us away from God. Or perhaps the evil one is simply using his authority over this fallen world to wreak havoc in our lives.

Hate the evil that Satan represents, but do not hate God.

Everything that happens in our lives and in the lives of our special children can be orchestrated by God to bring about good.

Aiden's problems arrived with a calling to a unique ministry. In the years since his birth, I have been afforded the opportunity to visit other mothers with newborns in the same situation, and I have published on the subject of his disability in many national publications, informing others of his type of defect. God has reached through this situation to benefit others and, in turn, to benefit Aiden.

Do I wish he didn't have this birth defect? Of course I do. But since he does, I rejoice in the fact that God can use us to help others.

There are higher purposes at work. God is taking the scattered pieces of your world and reshaping them into one in which you will be blessed and He will be glorified.

Prayer: Lord, You work all things for our good. Today I place my trust in that truth. Help me to answer this special calling You have placed on my life.

Pray Always

Praying always with all prayer and supplication in the Spirit.
—Ephesians 6:18

A friend of mine told me she shoots up arrow prayers all day long. In confusion, I asked what an "arrow prayer" was.

An arrow prayer is a quick prayer shot straight up just like an archer would shoot an arrow into the sky. The release is quick, and the arrow flies straight and is swallowed by the heavens. Arrow prayers fly quickly from our thoughts into the form of prayer and are released to the God of the heavens. They are not formal prayers with measured words. They are quick and informal.

Aaron ran in from playing outside. He dashed to his mother's side as she washed the lunch dishes. "Can we have a Popsicle?" he cried as he ran through the room. Before his mother could answer, he was back outside with his buddy.

His mother smiled at the little boy's enthusiasm and his belief that, since he asked, he would receive the Popsicle. She pulled out two—cherry-flavored, his favorite. His request was a quick "arrow" shot accurately to her benevolent nature.

Remember that God, who loves you more than anyone, wants to give you good things, too.

When your child struggles to get the spoon to her mouth, send up an arrow prayer of petition. When your child takes that first labored step, or mouths that first coherent word, send up an arrow prayer of thanksgiving. When you check on your sleeping child before going to bed, send up an arrow prayer of praise. When you lose your patience with your child and the struggles you both face, send up an arrow prayer of repentance—and another asking for God's patience.

Make a quick arrow prayer your immediate response to every situation in life. This is how we can live a prayer-filled and prayerful life.

Take the time for extended prayer, too. Arrow prayers are like quick chats. But nothing beats a long conversation with the One who loves you. If you are an early riser, take that morning time to spend with Him. Or if you prefer the night, spend those final moments in prayer before you go to sleep.

In between those times, keep sending up arrows. They are always caught.

Prayer: Help me to remember that I can always come to You in prayer . . . no matter how brief these prayers may be.

Weeping Mothers

A voice was heard in Ramah,
Lamentation, weeping, and great mourning,
Rachel weeping for her children,

Refusing to be comforted,
Because they are no more.

—Matthew 2:18

We are not the first mothers to weep over our children. Rachel and the women of her time wept over the children of Israel who were spirited away as slaves (Jer. 31:15). Again, in the time of Christ, the women of Israel sent up their tortured cries as evil destroyed their sons (Matt. 2:13–18).

Are you weeping over your child today? Do you grieve the loss of the child you had hoped for? Is the child you hold imperfect or dying?

When Rachel (and the women of Israel) are mentioned in the Bible, their grief is described, but they are not condemned for their outcry of pain. The Bible tells us that Rachel refuses to be comforted because of the loss. It doesn't say that she is acting out badly or should be accepting comfort.

Here is our permission to cry, to grieve, to feel the pain of our losses, to mourn. It is not unnatural. We are not told to hold it in.

Let it go. Cry out to God. Release the flood of tears. Give voice to your grief.

You may not be grieving the death or imminent death of your child. But you are grieving a loss that is just as valid when your child is born with a disability. The child that you grieve is the "normal" child of your dreams, the one you hoped for, the one you longed to hold and watch grow up. The one you had hoped would develop at the rate described in the charts printed in parenting magazines and books. The one that would behave like other children.

It is OK to grieve the loss of that dream.

God's shoulders are strong enough to cry on. His arms are warm enough to enfold you. And His compassion is steady enough to comfort you.

Join Rachel and all the mothers of Israel as they grieve their children. Don't hold it in. Give voice to your pain.

Prayer: Lord, the pain and sadness I feel over the loss of my dream are almost unbearable. Bring me the comfort only You can afford. I lift my grief to You.

Faith of a Child

But Jesus said, "Let the little children come to Me, and do not forbid them; for of such is the kingdom of heaven."
—Matthew 19:14

Jennifer had profound problems. After her adoption, her parents discovered she had cerebral palsy. Her tiny body was twisted and virtually useless. Her vocabulary consisted of a few sounds and monosyllabic words.

But her parents loved her and did whatever they could to ensure that Jennifer had a happy life. They also took the time to introduce her to Jesus and the church at a young age.

Each Sunday, Jennifer attended a Sunday school class with five other children. The teacher explained the lessons and chatted with the children. All the while, Jennifer listened attentively, smiling her bright, sunny smile that seemed to warm the room.

A few days before Jennifer was called home to be with the Lord, the topic of discussion was heaven. The teacher carefully explained heaven to the children, and a discussion ensued. One of the children expressed his fear of dying and leaving this life.

One by one the teacher asked the children if they would want to go to heaven and be with Jesus. Each one expressed some uncertainty and decided they would prefer to remain on earth for now.

Each one except Jennifer. She became more excited as the discussion continued. Finally the teacher turned to her and asked, "Would you be afraid to go to heaven, Jennifer?"

Laboring to express herself, Jennifer managed a somewhat garbled "No!"

Smiling, the teacher asked, "Why not?"

With glowing eyes and a beautiful expression on her face, Jennifer sang out clearly and distinctly, "Grandpa!"

Within weeks, Jennifer joined her beloved Grandpa in the presence of the Lord. The teacher is still moved by the faith and excitement Jennifer so clearly expressed.

Jennifer knew that she would be reunited with the loved ones she missed. She knew that heaven would be a wonderful place filled with love and laughter. She looked forward to it.

Prayer: Lord, help us to have the faith and excitement that Jennifer displayed. Help us to realize that this temporary place is not our true home.

✻ *Faith in What We Do Not See*

Now faith is the substance of things hoped for, the evidence of things not seen.

—Hebrews 11:1

Jody is godmother to a special-needs child. She prays diligently for him and visits when she can. Her commitment to this child is no less than the commitment she holds for each of her own four daughters.

One evening, while talking with the mother of her godson, Jody described the trials of life in this way:

Picture a huge ball of string. We take hold of one end of it and toss the other end far from us. The ball unravels and unravels. For a time we can see where the string is headed. But as the ball continues to roll, we lose sight of its path.

It may wind around a corner; it may become tangled for a moment; it may bounce to another level and roll easily down an incline. All we know is that the part of the string that we hold in our hand is not the complete ball of string. We see only a fragment, but the string continues onward.

Now picture your life—and the life of your child—as that same ball of string. You hold a fragment of that life in your hand. You live it today and know that it stretches out before you. You may not know the twists and turns that ball of string will take, but you know it is continuous. We also know that at some point in our life, the ball of string we cling to will bounce up to another level through death. And the string will continue onward.

If you concentrate on the little bit of string you hold, you miss out on so much that awaits you. Look forward, and see the string stretching out into eternity. Don't concentrate on the hardship of the tiny bit of string you hold in your hand. There is so much more to come. And once it bounces to the next level, the string unravels without hindrance.

Jody believes that the ball of string her godson holds is temporarily tangled in this life. It is not pretty at times, and it doesn't unravel smoothly. But she knows that at some time, his life will bounce to that other level, and this precious boy will continue his travels without difficulty throughout eternity.

Prayer: Lord, the little bit of string I hold is not the entire ball. You know the path the string of my life will take. I trust You to keep it rolling until I can bounce to the next level—life eternal with You—where there will be no hindrances.

A Gentle Shepherd for Mothers

And gently lead those who are with young.
—Isaiah 40:11

We can easily picture Jesus tenderly cradling a little lamb. It is easy to understand His love and tenderness for such a helpless creature.

Can you picture this truth from Scripture, that Jesus is just as gently leading you?

Picture that sheep of his flock. See the gentle shepherd moving the sheep through a rocky patch to the better grass on the other side. The rams and childless ewes race through the rocks with a small slip here and there. The shepherd lifts two bleating lambs, quieting their fears as he carries them across. Then he turns back, once again, to help one sheep through.

This sheep is frightened and unsure. Her little lamb is by her side and is too weak and afraid to cross the difficult pass. Softly coaxing them, the shepherd moves them one step at a time onto the dangerous stretch of ground. When the sheep falters or stumbles, he lifts her up, caresses her, gives her time to rest, and then gently prods her forward again. At times, over very difficult ground, he may lift her or her lamb and set them down again on another part of the path in order to continue their journey.

The sheep may not want to travel the path. She sees the rock; she senses the dangers. At times she may plant her feet and refuse to move. When she does, the gentle shepherd waits with her, tenderly assuring her that she is capable of the journey.

She does not know that, by traveling this difficult path, she will reach a place that is far better. The grass will be green and lush, her lamb will be free to frolic with the others, water will be plentiful, and the shepherd will be there to protect them from any future harm.

Are you this sheep? Are you afraid to move over the rocky ground, afraid of the pain and dangers it may bring? Listen to the quiet voice of the Shepherd who coaxes you forward. He has promised to be beside you, leading you gently to a better place for you and your child. He will not leave you to navigate the path alone.

Prayer: Thank You for Your daily guidance. I place my trust in You and step onto the path before me, knowing that You will travel with me. Lead me forward according to Your will.

He Holds the Lambs

He will feed His flock like a shepherd;
He will gather the lambs with His arm,
And carry them in His bosom.
                                        —Isaiah 40:11

It is a famous picture: Jesus walking with a shepherd's staff, cradling a small lamb in His arms.

Assign that lamb a name—give it the name of your child. Picture Jesus holding your little one, your lamb, in the same tender, caring manner. Your child is close enough to hear His heart beat, to feel His warmth and tender hands, and to listen to His soothing voice.

Jesus already holds your child in this manner. He has gathered your child with all of the differences, pain, and sorrows and is holding that precious little one close to His heart.

I think that Jesus holds these special children just a little closer. I believe He knows the special comfort and strength that they need from Him.

I think children with differences are the sweetest of the lambs in Jesus' flock. They may not be the most woolly or the most active, but they are the ones that receive His most tender care. They are the lambs that accept all the other lambs without turning away. They are the lambs that offer a sweet bleat when they see their mothers approaching. They are the special lambs in the field.

When these little lambs are weary or lost, Jesus cradles them in His loving arms and helps them along the way. In His arms, they can calm to the steady beat of His heart, a heart that is overflowing with love and tenderness for them. The lambs know this and will seek that love and comfort.

Do not worry, mother, if your special lamb is not in your care right now. He is in the arms of the Good Shepherd. Do not feel guilty when you need respite from the struggle. When you leave your child in the care of another, one set of caring arms is always present—those of the One who loves your baby more than anyone can.

Those loving arms will never leave your child. Jesus has gathered this little lamb close to His heart for eternity.

Prayer: Lord, thank You for the love You impart to my child. Hold my little lamb close to Your heart and keep this child safe in Your arms.

An Ovation of Love

This is My commandment, that you love one another as I have loved you.

—John 15:12

Three days before my son's first surgery, we stood before the people of our church family and dedicated him to the Lord. Aiden was just over two months old. We asked the members of the church to stand alongside us in our difficult journey and pray for our son and his surgeons. Ultimately, we placed him in the hands of God and submitted to His will. As part of the dedication ceremony, I sang a song as I held Aiden in my arms.

I stood at the microphone before more than a thousand people and lifted my voice. It was a song that had been running through my head since the day Aiden was born. I am sure that many expected a typical "baby dedication" song filled with words about the wonder of newly created life. That wonder was indeed valid, but the song God gave me had more to do with the situation we found ourselves in with a severely cleft-affected baby.

The song was "Be Ye Glad" by Michael Kelly Blanchard. It speaks of both struggle and release. In the final verse I inserted Aiden's name and sang of the truth that there is nothing that can ever separate him from the love of God. The song proclaimed my belief that Aiden is not a mistake, that he is a precious child of God who was given to me as a gift—no matter what the struggles involved in raising him.

And the song goes on to exhort me—and you—to be glad. There is nothing that can come between us and God's love for us! He has opened the cell door of our prison of sin! We are free and freely loved.

As I sang that final verse, the full impact of God's love hit me. My voice broke and tears poured from my eyes. I finished the song in a near whisper. For a moment there was silence.

Then applause started. Applause like I had never heard before nor have ever heard since. It grew to a roar as one by one the people of my Christian family stood. This ovation wasn't for my singing; I had not sung well. This ovation was the embodiment of God's love flowing through His Church to engulf and overwhelm one small woman who needed to know its reality. Hundreds of men and women stood weeping with me in a communion of love and fellowship like I have never experienced at any other time.

It was a taste of God's heaven right here on earth.

Prayer: Lord, thank You for the Church on earth, Your hands in human form. You show us Your love for us through them in so many ways. Help me to be Your love and help to others in the Church when they need to know Your love is real.

A Blessing

> *Behold, children are a heritage from the LORD,*
> *The fruit of the womb is a reward.*
>
> —Psalm 127:3

Your child is a gift, a reward! Rejoice in the life of this little one because it is a blessing, because it is a gift, because it is eternal! This present struggle is a mere breath compared to the eternity your child will have to dance and sing and play in the presence of God!

I like the end of Psalm 127:3 because it says children are a reward—all children.

It doesn't say "perfect children" are a reward. Or "healthy children." Or "children with dark skin . . . children with light skin . . . children with straight hair . . . children with curly hair . . . children with blue eyes or brown eyes or green eyes . . . children who can see or hear or speak . . . children who have superior intelligence . . . children with whole bodies . . . children with musical ability . . . children who can run or leap or throw a ball . . . perfect children."

It simply says "children." *All* children. My child. Your child. Every child.

Every child on this earth is a special gift from God, a blessing He saw fit to give to the right parents. There are no accidents—God knows what He is doing. He searched through all eternity for the exact parents for this little child you hold. God chose you and placed His reward in your arms.

Your child is not his or her disability. My child is not a cleft or a series of surgeries. He is a little boy who loves and laughs and blesses my life. Our children are defined by the fact that they are image-bearers of God—made in His image. Their value is in the importance placed upon them by the God of the universe—so important that He died for them too.

Look beyond the differences. See the reward.

Prayer: Lord, You know the perfect timing of each step in Your eternal plan. Help me to see my child as You do: as a reward, a gift, and a blessing . . . no matter what problems may be present.

Lonely but Not Alone

My loved ones and my friends stand aloof from my plague,
And my relatives stand afar off.

—Psalm 38:11

It is human nature to avoid situations with which we are uncomfortable. You may have noticed it with your friends now that you have a child with special needs. Those who were so helpful in the early days after the birth of your child may not be coming around quite so often now. Some may have faded from your life altogether.

Part of the reason is that they may not know what to say or do. They cannot relate to the upheaval of life that you are experiencing. They may have very mixed emotions about your child, just as you do. They may be sad, angry, afraid, and happy all at the same time but are unaware of which emotion is "appropriate" to express. So they solve the dilemma by not having to deal with it at all . . . by avoiding you and your child.

Perhaps part of the reason you may not see your friends as often is because of their fear that this could be their own child. "There but for the grace of God . . ." may be a refrain that resounds in their heads. They feel relief that it isn't them, but then feel guilty for thinking that. Or maybe the changes in your life have made you unavailable to them. The demands of a special-needs child can be all-encompassing, taking over much of your time. Maybe your change of lifestyle simply means you have outgrown certain friends with whom you have little in common anymore.

Whatever the reason, loneliness is very real and very hard. King David certainly felt it. He told of how his situation and loneliness made his strength fail and the light fade from his eyes. He must have been angry that he was avoided because of his wounds. You might feel some of that same anger. It helps you cope with the loneliness and longing.

Try to think through the situation clearly. The desire for the companionship of other Christians is natural and necessary. See if you can determine what is keeping your friends at bay. Are they afraid? Ask them, and begin an open dialogue about those fears. Give them permission to express their mixed emotions. Let them know it is normal.

Are you unavailable? Perhaps once a week or every other week your spouse or a friend could watch your child while you meet with a few friends for a walk, a dinner, or some other activity. Make the evening fun—you can even make a rule that no "serious" talk is allowed for that one evening. Invite a friend over for coffee while your little one naps so that you can give your undivided attention.

No matter what, remember that you are not really alone. There is a God who walks beside you every step you take. He sits with you and eats with you. He loves you. Talk to Him throughout your day. He is there with you right now.

Prayer: Lord, I am lonely today. Be my companion and my comfort. Teach me how to depend fully on You while helping me to see ways in which I can be a friend to others.

The Grace to Be Humble

God resists the proud,
But gives grace to the humble.
*—*1 Peter 5:5

Sometimes it is difficult to be a receiver of blessings, especially if you are an active giver. Some of the most difficult moments in raising a child with special needs can be when someone offers you assistance or prayer.

Georgie has always been a go-getter. She has served the people of her church faithfully. Whenever there was a baby born or an illness, she was one of the first to deliver a meal or send a gift. If she knew that a ministry need was unfulfilled, Georgie would find a way to fill it either by volunteering herself or finding someone who was willing to serve.

Georgie loves serving. It is her gift.

What she isn't so good at is being served herself. When Georgie's son was born with several physical defects, she was overwhelmed with the responsibility of caring for him and her two other children. But Georgie didn't ask for help. She struggled through her days feeling stressed and angry.

Others in the church and in her neighborhood offered their assistance, but Georgie refused. She simply could not humble herself to be on the receiving end of the kindnesses she had so faithfully given over the years.

Georgie was too proud to receive.

One afternoon Georgie's neighbor brought over some coffee and rolls. She sat Georgie down at the kitchen table and, while cradling the baby in her arms, asked Georgie why she was refusing the help offered by so many. Georgie couldn't find a valid answer until she realized it was her own pride at being the giver rather than the receiver.

"Don't you know that when you allow another person to do something for you, they in turn receive a blessing?" her neighbor asked. "So you are doing something for them too. You allow them to be blessed, you help strengthen their ability to serve, and you allow them that wonderful feeling that comes from helping others."

Georgie repented of her prideful refusals and began to receive the gifts of love offered her and her child. Immediately she felt a strong sense of peace and knew that God was pleased. And as time passed she was able to pass on what she learned to others as well.

Prayer: Lord, help me not to be proud, but to humbly receive the gifts You send my way through others.

But It's Impossible

Because it is written, "Be holy, for I am holy."
—1 Peter 1:16

The Scriptures seem to be full of impossible requirements, orders we are given to follow that we simply can never really fulfill.

Take, for example, this verse from Ephesians (5:25): "Husbands, love your wives, just as Christ also loved the church and gave Himself for her." Impossible! No one could ever come close to loving the way Christ does, right?

Wrong. When God tells us to be holy as He is, or to love as He does, or forgive as He does, He is not setting us up to fail at an impossible task! On the contrary, He is giving us our marching orders *and* giving us the ability to complete our task *through His power!*

We cannot be holy on our own, but God makes us holy and set apart when we receive Him. We cannot love as He does unless we surrender to Him and allow Him to love through us. We cannot forgive as He does unless He is allowed lordship over our hearts and minds.

God would never tell us to do something that is impossible. So when we are given a task that seems impossible, we must realize that God is teaching us to depend on Him.

In the same way, He would never have gifted you with a special child unless He knew it was the best thing for your path in life. And with this gift, He gives the strength and ability to carry on *through Him.* We need only learn to rely on His grace and power to sustain us and guide us as we raise our children.

We must surrender to Him and allow Him the freedom to fill us with His strength and love. We can do this! We can raise our wonderful children with love and perseverance.

You can do it, mother! There are thousands of us cheering you on! And there is a mighty God standing with you every moment of every day. His grace is there for the asking.

Prayer: Lord, I have my marching orders. What seems impossible for me is not impossible for You. I look to You to be my guide and partner in raising my child.

Following His Example

Imitate me, just as I also imitate Christ.
—1 Corinthians 11:1

Sarah's mother was not concerned about her daughter's speech difficulties. After all, Sarah has Pierre Robin syndrome, which is characterized by a horseshoe-shaped cleft in the soft palate and a "floppy" tongue. Sarah's daddy has the same syndrome and speaks perfectly well. It was assumed that with surgery and therapy, Sarah would learn to speak just fine.

When Sarah was almost two, she joined a language group in which she would interact with other children her age as they practiced their speaking skills.

It was in this class that Sarah's mother met little Aaron. Aaron had been born with most of his mouth missing. But after two surgeries, Aaron spoke quite well. He had been working twice a month with a dedicated speech therapist and practiced daily with his mother.

When Sarah's mother heard Aaron speak, she became motivated to teach Sarah to speak just as clearly. She dedicated more time to practice and became more involved with her therapy. Seeing the ability Aaron displayed was inspirational, and Sarah's mother decided to follow the example of Aaron's mother and Aaron himself.

Following the example of others can be healthy. It can give hope and revive your commitment to persevere. However, becoming too dependent on the example of others can also be devastating. It can lead to disappointment, jealousy, and resentment if we try to push our children to follow perfectly the examples of other children.

We cannot drive our children to achieve standards others may set. We need to learn our child's individual limitations and then help them to develop into the wonderful person God created them to be—without damaging comparisons to other human beings. The only example we should focus our efforts on is that of Christ.

Paul knew this and encouraged others to follow his example as he followed the example of Christ. He didn't say, "Do as I do, because I am perfect." Rather he recognized that the real example to follow is that of Christ. The Lord has set an example to which we can truly aspire.

Prayer: Lord, thank You for the unique qualities of my child. Help me to build him up, teaching him to realize the potential You planted within him.

Foolishness

> *The way of a fool is right in his own eyes,*
> *But he who heeds counsel is wise.*
> —Proverbs 12:15

A speech therapist for the county's Early Intervention program tenderly tells the story of one of her little clients. The child, Noah, loves to play with the therapist's Winnie the Pooh toy figurines, which come in a little tree house with tiny furniture and several of the famous characters.

Every visit, Noah dumps out the toys and begins setting up the kitchen with its little table and four little chairs. And every visit, without fail, Noah attempts to sit on one of the chairs.

Noah is an average-sized two-year-old. The chair is about three inches high. Obviously, Noah's attempts have never been successful.

But Noah, due to his disability, still thinks that he can fit into the tiny chair. And he will probably continue to try to do so over the next year. He innocently believes that his attempts are fine. No matter how often Noah is told he does not fit in the chair, he must try it for himself.

How often are we like Noah, trying to follow our own way when evidence mounts against our behavior?

It is easy to allow trying circumstances to become an excuse to choose the wrong way to cope—easing our fears with food or alcohol or by staying too busy. These methods may seem right to us at the time—we may feel we "deserve" a vice or two considering the difficulties we face. But God is clear about the use of anything to cope outside of dependence on Him. He has given His Word, the Bible, to advise us and teach us. He has given us the Church to provide fellowship and support. He has given His Spirit to convict us and enable us to continue. Our obligation is to accept what He provides.

Prayer: Lord, help me not to be foolish, but to turn to You for advice and direction in my life. Help me to remember that the only true aid comes from You through Your Word, Your Spirit, and Your Church.

Train Up Your Child

Train up a child in the way he should go,
And when he is old he will not depart from it.
—Proverbs 22:6

Three-year-old Allison was facing a major surgery in two weeks. One of her therapists brought her a "surgery gift," a stuffed bear with a cassette recorder imbedded deep in the plush body. It came with several story tapes pertaining to disability, surgery, hope, and death.

Allison was thrilled with her bear. In fact, she was so taken with the new toy that she had trouble concentrating on her therapy session. Finally her mother put the bear back in the box. She told Allison to tell the bear "night-night" because he needed a nap until the therapist was finished.

Allison whispered, "Ni-ni," and then knelt beside the box containing the bear. To her mother's surprise and delight, Allison folded her hands and began to pray, "Now I lay me down to sleep . . ."

It was obvious to those present, and to those who heard about it later, that Allison was being raised to pray. She felt no shame about taking a break in the middle of a therapy session to reach out in prayer on behalf of her new friend. She lifted her voice in the purity of her child-faith and called upon the Lord, knowing He heard her.

What a beautiful example of a mother training up her child in the way that she should go! And, because of this mother's training, Allison was able to call upon her fledgling faith in an appropriate moment.

What hope and confirmation must have filled the heart of that mother!

Each of us can use this example as encouragement to continue training up our children to trust the Lord. The dependence we display will help our children to depend on Him throughout their lives. The priority we set on prayer and time in the Bible will not be missed by those little ones.

And one day we, too, may be rewarded by a spontaneous act of faith from our child.

Prayer: Lord, thank You for the purity of heart that little children possess. Help me to be diligent and joyful in the training of my child so that one day this little one may follow You with complete trust.

Dancing Before the Lord

Michal, Saul's daughter, looked through a window and saw King David leaping and whirling before the LORD; and she despised him in her heart.

—2 Samuel 6:16

My daughter Kaitlynne loved to go to church services. She especially loved the praise and worship portion of the service during which the congregation sang and clapped. Kaitlynne would sit in the back of the building in an aisle seat. This enabled Kaitlynne the freedom to dance to the music. She would spin and leap and enjoy the atmosphere of praise.

She never bumped anyone else, and she always stayed near me. Most people would watch the child's exuberant praise with smiles. A few, however, would frown disapproval. After a time this disapproval caused me to feel shame over my child's dance. Eventually I made Kaitlynne sit quietly in a chair beside me.

One morning, Kaitlynne slipped from her chair and began dancing in the aisle. As I turned to scold her, the pastor walked in from the back of the church. He placed his hand on Kaitlynne's golden-brown hair and prayed a blessing for her. He looked into my eyes and said, "If only we could all be so free in our praise! I miss seeing this little girl dancing every Sunday. It has been an inspiration to me of the freedom we have in the Lord."

Kaitlynne now dances each Sunday in the aisle at the back of the church, her method of praising the God she loves to visit in His special house.

Centuries ago, King David danced with joyous abandon before the ark of the covenant when it was brought to Jerusalem. His wife looked out the window with disapproval and shame. She took David to task over it. He explained that he was dancing in celebration before the Lord. And his wife, because of her disapproval, had no children to the day of her death.

Does your little one cause you to feel embarrassed when he or she makes noise in Sunday service? Do others give you those "why can't you keep that child quiet?" type of looks? Take heart, mother. If your child is dancing or singing or shouting in praise to the Lord, you can celebrate with her.

Allow your child and yourself the freedom to praise with

abandon. Get a praise CD and play it at home while you dance and leap together before the Lord. Dance for your child to watch. Sing and clap your hands. Make a joyful noise. Allow your little one to feel the vibrations of the music. Enjoy God together!

Prayer: Lord, thank You for the freedom You offer in worship. Help us to praise You without shame.

Don't Forget to Laugh

> *A time to weep,*
> *And a time to laugh;*
> *A time to mourn,*
> *And a time to dance.*
> —Ecclesiastes 3:4

Hopefully you have taken the time to grieve over the struggles you face with your child. The Lord tells us that there are appropriate times to weep and mourn. The sadness over your child's problems is normal, and expressing that with tears is healthy.

But don't allow your mourning to erase laughter from your life. Your child, no matter what the problems or special needs, will be a source of joy for you at times.

If your child does something silly or funny, laugh! You aren't making fun of your little one, you are celebrating the fun he brings to your life.

Aiden is a clown. He loves to be the center of attention and to make people laugh. However, many times he is incredibly funny when he doesn't mean to be—all children are!

At the age of two, Aiden attended a speech and language group. His first day in the class he was toddling about, exploring the room. During his travels he passed a mirror positioned low enough for the children to see themselves full-length. Aiden passed it, did a double take, and yelled out, "Hey! Aben!! (his word for Aiden)." He backed up and began dancing before the mirror, chanting his own name, "Aben! Aben! Aben! Aben!" Class came to a halt until the teachers could stop laughing. They weren't making fun of a disabled child, they were enjoying the wonderful spontaneity of a little boy discovering himself in a mirror.

Later that summer the class was practicing the sound for the letter *p*. As a project, they were finger painting with pudding. Aiden sat down with his paper and promptly ate his pudding. He then proceeded to eat the pudding belonging to the little girl on the right, followed by the pudding on his left. Then, when no other puddings were in reach, he got up and traveled around the table, stealing tastes of pudding from each bowl. His teachers were in stitches again. (His mother was not in the room, or the pudding theft would have been stopped sooner.)

What funny things has your child been up to? Laugh. Enjoy your child. Allow others to enjoy her antics. There is nothing so satisfying as laughter!

At the end of each day, spend a moment recalling the precious moments of the day—the laughter, the smiles, the hugs. It will help turn the time of weeping into a time of laughter and the time of mourning into dancing.

Prayer: Lord, help me to see the funny things my child does each day. Turn my weeping to laughter, my mourning to dancing. Show me the joy living in my child.

Giving to Ease Another's Pain

> Your prayers and your alms have come
> up for a memorial before God.
> —Acts 10:4

A family in our city lost their son to death when he was under three years old. He needed a heart and lung transplant, but no organs were received in time to save his mortal life. The family retreated in pain to grieve their precious son.

After a time, this family began reaching out to others in order to help ease their grief. They became active donors to the Early Intervention program that had helped their son during his young life. They provided learning toys and other items desperately needed by the therapists on their home visits. Many little children will learn new concepts and speech while using the toys this family provided.

Both parents began speaking publicly on the importance of organ donation. Thanks to their efforts, many people have signed their driver's licenses to indicate a desire to donate their organs in the event of death. Countless lives will be affected by their advocacy.

When they heard of a family with nine children, all of whom slept on the floor in sleeping bags, they provided a bed. They insisted that a bed must have bedding, so they also purchased new sheets and blankets to go along with their gift. The mother asked the social worker involved with the family if they needed a couple of pillows too. When she found out that none of the children had pillows, nine pillows joined the pile of gifts.

This mother acts out of her recognition of the pain of others. She knows what it is like to hurt on behalf of one's child. So she spends time trying to ease that pain in some little way for another mother. All of her actions are anonymous.

And she will be the first to admit that her works help her to deal with her own pain. She does not escape it with her actions, but she does find joy in helping others. It is one link in the long healing process through which she travels.

Each of us, in this unique group of mothers with special-needs children, can understand this type of pain like no one else. We can be a lifeline and a help to each other. Is there some way in which you can help another woman in her journey? Are there children whom you can help out with a gift or your time?

Reaching out is the next step in healing.

Prayer: Lord, help me to recognize the needs of others. Give me the resources and the discernment needed to help in some small way.

The Anchor Holds

This hope we have as an anchor of the soul, both sure and steadfast.

—Hebrews 6:19

Ray Boltz wrote and recorded a song called "The Anchor Holds." After Aiden's birth, I was seized with an incredible need to find that recording and purchase it. Over and over through my day the phrase "the anchor holds" would repeat in my thoughts.

A friend of mine who is purchaser for a Christian bookstore ordered Boltz's CD for me. Before it was delivered, a friend called to tell me she kept picturing an anchor and felt the need to encourage me with the truth that God is as steadying as an anchor.

As I spoke with her on the telephone, my four-year-old son called me in obvious distress. "It's stuck, Mommy. Help me!" I turned to see that he had been playing with a little boat that had a plastic anchor on a string. Somehow he had tangled the anchor in a child-gate. As I bent to untangle it, a process that lasted close to fifteen minutes, I was struck again with the strength of that symbol. (God was making it very clear to me that He is my Anchor!)

An anchor not only holds a ship steady, it will save lives in a storm. It will keep ships from crashing into rocks or each other. It will keep them firmly in one place. The anchor will help a ship stay where its work is to be accomplished.

God is that firm Anchor when we are tossed in the stormy seas of life. He will steady us and save us from crashing. He will keep us firmly in one place—where our work is to be accomplished.

When I received the CD, I was amazed to read in the jacket notes that a verse of the song is written about a tiny premature infant who died. More and more I could feel God's message clearly stated: He is my Anchor. The song proved it and even alluded to the difficulty of having a child with problems. The phone call proved it. My child's toy was even used to "anchor" the message in my heart.

During each surgery, I rely on that Anchor to hold me steady and help me through. Each day He is my mainstay and my mooring. I need only trust in His firm grip and believe that He will keep me steady.

Prayer: Lord, You are my Anchor, my Rock, and my Stronghold. I depend on You to be my strength and to hold me firm during the storms of life. Thank You for the hope that trusting You instills in my heart.

A Cheerful Face

> *A merry heart makes a cheerful countenance,*
> *But by sorrow of the heart the spirit is broken.*
>
> —Proverbs 15:13

Bonnie's son had serious heart problems. He was snatched from her arms after birth and flown to another city for treatment. Bonnie, still weak from a difficult delivery, checked herself out of the hospital and followed him.

For weeks, Bonnie slept on a cot just off the pediatric intensive care unit while her little one struggled for life. She was heartbroken, tired, and stressed out.

Seeing the plight of the mothers visiting the children in the unit, the nurses, with incredible compassion, worked to lighten their heavy hearts. Each crib and machine sported bright decorations and little signs heralding weight gains or other accomplishments. During the night, while the mothers slept, the nurses would dress the babies in little costume bibs and hats according to the season. They would snap a Polaroid photograph, undress the child, and then display the photograph on the crib for the mother to find.

Bonnie had cried most of the night. In the morning she walked over to her baby's crib to check on him. She was greeted by a photograph of her son dressed as a leprechaun. His face was squinched up in disapproval. On the photograph was a caption reading, "I don't want to be a leprechaun!" Bonnie smiled.

A nurse approached her and gently whispered, "That's the first time you've smiled. Feels good, doesn't it?"

To Bonnie's surprise, it did feel good. She credits that moment with a turning in her outlook. She began to look for other reasons to smile, and to help other mothers smile. Eventually, she was able to do the same for her husband and other children. Her heart's burden seemed less heavy, and she could smile and laugh again.

Is there something keeping you from smiling today? Studies have shown that laughter can be a great source of healing. Look at your world: Isn't there something there that can bring a smile to your face? Perhaps you can call a friend who always lightens your mood, or list your blessings, or read a funny book, or listen to a funny tape. And, in turn, share some of the fun moments with someone else who may need a smile—your spouse, your children, your extended family, or your friends. It will help to lighten your spirit.

Prayer: Lord, although I have much to be unhappy about, I know there is much in which to rejoice. Thank You for the moments of happiness and smiles You bring to me each day. Help me to focus my thoughts on them when times are difficult.

The Cuddlers

Love suffers long and is kind; love does not envy; love does not parade itself, is not puffed up; does not behave rudely, does not seek its own . . . [love] bears all things, believes all things, hopes all things, endures all things. Love never fails.

—1 Corinthians 13:4–5, 7–8

They are angels to me, the cuddlers. They tiptoe into the hospital room and ask to hold my child so that I may eat a meal or take a brief moment of respite. I turn in the doorway and look back to see my child snuggled against an ample bosom, rocking while a gentle song caresses him.

These women come in many forms: teenagers, young mothers, and grandmothers. They walk from room to room or wait in the lounge area of the pediatric wing of the hospital, waiting to hold a baby or play with a child so that a tired mother can have a moment out of the sterile room, comforted in knowing her child is safe and cuddled and unafraid. These women spend hours trying to give that little bit of comfort to women they have never met.

The cuddlers are not paid for their services. They volunteer to be there on one of the most difficult wings of the hospital because they love the children. Because they love the suffering mothers. Because they love to serve others.

They ask for no reward; they receive no money for their time. They are embarrassed if I try to tell them what a blessing they have been to me and my son.

The cuddlers are the embodiment of God's love. They hold my child, protecting him and loving him with the arms of God. Their soft songs are the voice of God giving comfort to my hurting child . . . and to me.

When God rewards those who have served on earth, I think the cuddlers will have the most beautiful of crowns, covered with small, sparkling jewels, one for each of the small children they loved for those brief moments in the hospital.

We can share in the love of the cuddlers by passing on their legacy: reaching out to another hurting soul with no expectation of return.

Prayer: Lord, thank You for the cuddlers. Bless these giving women as they reach out and show Your love to those who are suffering. Help me to bring Your love to a hurting world just as the cuddlers do.

Day by Day

This is the day the LORD has made;
We will rejoice and be glad in it.
—Psalm 118:24

Zachary probably will not live through another year. This frail ten-year-old has an inoperable brain tumor. His headaches are a bit more frequent now, and his body is weaker. But he still has a hundred-watt smile and an easy laugh. He gives his mommy the best hugs in the world.

Zachary's mother is tired. She is tired of the battle, she is tired of the chemotherapy, and she is tired of seeing her boy in pain. But she fights on, trying to make Zachary's last days as pain-free and fun-filled as possible.

"We live day by day. We wake up each morning and thank God for the day we have. We have a lot to be thankful for." She smiles and tousles the wispy hair on her son's head. Then she begins to list the blessings.

"We've had Zachary with us for ten years. He makes us laugh. He is so smart and funny. He draws pictures and writes us notes. Today, Zachary saw a cardinal outside his window on a pine tree." He grins and nods, excited at the memory.

Zachary's mother knows that she will not always have her son by her side, so she sees each day as another precious span of time during which she can be with him. She tries to focus on just that one day, not looking ahead with fear or dread. One day. One day at a time.

And each day yields moments of blessing and laughter. Each evening they pray together, thanking the Lord for one more day . . . and hoping for another.

"I know the day will come to grieve, but why grieve now? Zachary is here now. We are together today. So we try to make each day fun. God gave us today. He doesn't promise us tomorrow."

She speaks easily of her belief that no matter when Zachary leaves this life, he will live on with the Lord until the two of them can be reunited.

Until that time, they rejoice in each day the Lord has made.

Prayer: Lord, thank You for the day You have given me. Help me to take on the struggle one day at a time. Help me to see each day as a precious gift that You have made.

Step into Descent

And it shall come to pass, as soon as the soles of the feet of the priests who bear the ark of the LORD, the Lord of all the earth, shall rest in the waters of the Jordan, that the waters of the Jordan shall be cut off, the waters that come down from upstream, and they shall stand as a heap.

—Joshua 3:13

Joshua received the order to go up into the promised land after years of wandering in the desert. The only obstacle in the way was the Jordan River. It is interesting to know that the name Jordan means "descent." To descend is to go down. So Joshua and the Israelites had to step into "descent"; only then would the water stop so that they could move forward into the promised land.

It was a step of faith. They had to step in, trusting that the Lord would halt the icy water. They had to suffer the descent before they could go upward.

Jacob had to be held down by three nurses during his last shot. He is so tired of doctors poking him and hurting him. He knows that the shot is helpful and will help to make him well. But it hurts. His mother helps to hold him, knowing this step of descent, in the long run, will actually allow her son to step upward.

Aiden does not understand why he falls asleep in his mother's arms and awakens hooked up to machines and in pain. He doesn't know that the surgeries he must undergo will help him to speak more clearly, eat more easily, and hear more distinctly. He just knows that something happened and now he is in pain. His mother, with an aching yet hopeful heart, once again signs the papers to allow the surgeon to work on her son. Her child is stepping into descent in order to step upward.

Sarah bravely watches the monitors as the chemicals slip into her bloodstream. She knows that in a few hours she will be sick and drained of energy. She knows that more of her hair will fall out tomorrow. But she knows that the chemotherapy is working. The tumor in her chest, which was the size of her daddy's fist, is now the size of a pea. She steps into descent, almost ready to take that step upward.

We, like Joshua all those years ago, must step out in faith every day of our lives while raising our special children. We pray, study our options, talk to physicians, and then step into descent so that our child can move forward. Sometimes descent may take the form of painful procedures that will help our children in the long run. Sometimes descent is doing nothing, watching our child remain the same or slip further away. We may sink into an emotional or spiritual descent.

But take hope, mother. There will come a day when we pass through that Jordan River and emerge on the other side to step upward into the presence of the Lord. And we may begin that upward journey today, right here on earth, as we step forward trusting Him.

Prayer: Today I step forward, trusting You to lift me and my child upward in Your time.

Jesus Wept

Jesus wept.
—John 11:35

There is nothing more profound to me than the meaning behind this short verse. Jesus had arrived at the tomb of His friend. He had seen the grieving of the dead man's sisters, who were also friends of His. He had seen the other mourners. He knew of their accusations that He could have saved the man from dying. He knew others believed the same thing yet made no accusations. He saw the faith of many of those near Him. He knew what He was about to do. He was surrounded by people.

Yet Jesus stood before the tomb of Lazarus and wept.

We may not know exactly what prompted His tears—the death of His friend, the grief of Mary and Martha, the lack of faith of some, or any combination of these things. But we do know the Lord stood and openly wept.

I take comfort in this verse, in knowing that crying is natural and acceptable to God. He not only gives us permission to do so, He demonstrated the appropriateness of it.

When my own child is hurting after a surgery, he lifts his chubby arms up to me so that I will lift him from his crib and cuddle him. He snuggles in under my chin, his dimpled fingers clutching the front of my shirt, and he will cry. I rock him and kiss the top of his blond head and brush away his tears. I whisper how much I love him and that everything will be OK soon. I sing him a song of my own making, filled with love and tenderness. And I hold him closer until the pain stops and he can rest.

When you are hurting, reach your arms up to the Lord so that He can lift you up and hold you close. Snuggle into the protective arms of *Abba*, a term that is the equivalent of "Daddy." Reach out and clutch His robe and cry. He will tenderly rock you and kiss the top of your head and brush away your tears. He will whisper how much He loves you. He will tell you that everything will be OK soon. He will sing to you a song of His own making filled with love and tenderness. He will hold you close until the pain stops and you can rest.

The Lord longs to hold you when you cry. He longs to give comfort and healing to your heavy heart. He longs to reassure you and give you peace.

Open your heart to Him. Weep openly before the Lord.

Prayer: Lord, hold me when I cry. Comfort me and wipe away my tears. I come to You because no one else can ease this pain inside. I cry out to You, and You hear me. Thank You for Your tender compassion and love.

Clothed in Compassion

Therefore, as the elect of God, holy and beloved, put on tender mercies, kindness, humility of mind, meekness, longsuffering.
—Colossians 3:12

Peggy was pregnant with twins when she and her husband, Ed, heard the joyful news that Ed's sister, Shirley, was also pregnant. She dreamed of the three children growing up together, playing and laughing, becoming confidants and conspirators. She could picture the children together at family gatherings and in school. She called Shirley each day, and the two shared many hopes and dreams.

Those dreams ended when Peggy's twins entered the world too soon. The first died right away. The second fragile baby fought for only a few short hours before joining the first. Peggy was overcome with grief. She returned home to an empty house, walking through the rooms that would never echo with the sounds of her twins.

She and Ed began to reconstruct their shattered world. Her calls to Shirley continued, as Peggy prayed fervently for the safety of her sister-in-law's baby.

One evening the wonderful news came—along with a heart-stopping blow: Shirley had labored all day and delivered *twins*. It was a shock to all, including the doctor.

Peggy had a choice. She could avoid the new babies, thereby avoiding the painful reminder of her two heaven-dwelling babies. Or she could clothe herself in kindness and humility.

Peggy chose the latter. Moreover, realizing the difficulty a new mother of twins can face, Peggy packed up her belongings and moved into Shirley's house to help out until Shirley could handle the babies on her own.

Peggy doesn't claim to know why her babies died and Shirley's lived. But she does know that God expects us to live a life of love and compassion. So when she saw Shirley's need, Peggy acted in the manner she believed God would expect of her. And she was rewarded with the joy of watching her two nephews grow into fine young men.

Prayer: Sometimes the old cliché comes to mind: "When you're handed lemons, make lemonade." Lord, help me to take the bitter lemon of life and sweeten it with compassionate kindness and love.

Like a Little Child

Assuredly, I say to you, whoever does not receive the kingdom of God as a little child will by no means enter it.

—Mark 10:15

A person with a mental disability may be very childlike in their outlook on the world. They may take any statement literally, they may have childish fears, and many can be as narcissistic as a two-year-old.

But God can use these beautifully pure hearts to do His work. Often they are willing to follow His leading and are less likely to succumb to fear or embarrassment.

Wayne, a residential care worker, was having a bad day. His

personal life was in turmoil, and he carried that stress with him to work. Wayne works with mentally handicapped adults. And, although Wayne tried to hide his inner distress, one of the residents recognized it.

Walking over to Wayne, the resident asked why he was so sad. Wayne looked up in surprise, which became shock as he recognized the man who was speaking to him. This resident was one of the more selfish of all those in the home. Leaning close to Wayne, the man continued in a whisper, "It will be OK."

As he shuffled away, another worker who had witnessed the exchange hurried over to Wayne. They both spoke excitedly about the resident's capability to connect with Wayne's emotional state and his desire to comfort Wayne.

Wayne has thought long and hard about the incident, formulating his belief in God's work in and through those who have a mental disability. He says, "I do think that many times mentally handicapped people have a deeper understanding of emotion. In this case, I know that God was using him to assure me that God is still in control."

This illustrates the truth that God can and will use any willing vessel, no matter how damaged or uneducated, to reach out to us in love.

Prayer: Lord, thank You for the purity of the childlike mind. Help me to be childlike in my faith, receiving whatever You have to give with a grateful heart. And help me to give to others in the same faithful manner.

Looking Beyond the Surface

For man looks at the outward appearance,
but the LORD looks at the heart.
                    —1 Samuel 16:7

Kaitlynne was in second grade when her class visited the school's counseling department for a unit on disabilities awareness. No one in Kaitlynne's class was disabled. However, her little brother, age eighteen months, was disabled.

The class discussed various disabilities and how everyone can learn from and interact with those who are differently abled. The children eagerly offered their input, several demonstrating a serious lack of understanding.

The counselor paused and then asked the children to raise their hands if they knew anyone with a disability. No one raised a hand. The counselor scanned the eager faces before her, finally resting her eyes on Kaitlynne. "Kaitlynne, do you know anyone with a disability?" Kaitlynne frowned and thought a moment. Then she shook her head. "Are you sure?" prompted the counselor. Again, Kaitlynne responded in the negative.

The counselor, slightly frustrated, leaned closer. "What about your little brother?"

Kaitlynne smiled brightly. "Oh no, he doesn't have a disability! He just has different problems than me!" She went on to describe how fun and loving her little brother is, not once mentioning the disability.

How wonderful Kaitlynne's answer was! In her eyes, there is nothing more "wrong" with her little brother than with any other human being—he just has a different set of problems. She was essentially blind to the physical problem, but saw clearly the wonderful little boy that is her brother.

Kaitlynne was looking at her little brother in the same manner the Lord looks at us. He does not look at our outward appearance or our physical problems. He doesn't see exceptional physical beauty and rank that person on a higher level of value. He doesn't see deformity or obesity and rank that person on a lower level of value. He looks far deeper. The Lord sees the heart, the innermost being.

We all stand on equal footing before the Lord: the whole, the misshapen, the genius, the mentally challenged. Each one is equally valued and loved. Each one is desired and sought out for personal relationship. Each one is judged solely on the motivation and action of the heart.

Prayer: Thank You for looking past the physical and seeing only what is truly important. We are all equal in Your eyes and truly valued. Help me to remember that truth.

Calming the Fear

And say to him: "Take heed, and be quiet; do not fear or be fainthearted."
—Isaiah 7:4

Grace was terrified. Her baby had been taken to a different hospital, and she had only just arrived there. She hadn't yet seen her little one, and no one could give her answers as to her baby's condition. She sat in a small room waiting for the pediatric cardiologist to see her. She tried to pray, but words just would not form. She stood up to pace, but three steps were all that was needed to traverse the entire room. She sat down again, wringing her hands. She picked up a magazine and flipped through the pages without seeing them.

Finally, the doorknob turned. Grace's heart began beating wildly, fear almost choking her. The door opened and in stepped the cardiologist. The first thing Grace noticed was his brightly colored Micky Mouse tie. The dancing figures of the famous cartoon characters smiled out at her with what she describes as reassurance. Her heartbeat slowed, and she felt a new sense of peace.

Lifting her eyes to the man's face, Grace saw sparkling blue eyes under a shock of white hair. The doctor sat on the chair across from her and took her hand. Grace doesn't remember much of what he said that day, but she remembers him saying that her baby was going to be OK. There would be treatments and possibly surgery, but eventually everything would be all right. He would not be the same as many other children: he would be a bit smaller, a little slower, a bit different—but he would be OK.

She remembers those words . . . and that tie.

It took that little cheerful reminder to jolt her into remembering that God was in control. She recalled that God does not give us a spirit of fear, but one of power and strength. She just needed a nudge in the form of a colorful Mickey Mouse tie. It said to her, "Don't be afraid; don't lose heart."

So often, we can give in to that spirit of fear, forgetting for a time that God can handle our situation, that He can provide peace in the midst of the most difficult circumstances. When we do give in to fear, God is faithful to send us reminders through His people, our surroundings, and His Word. When you feel anxiety threaten to overtake you, remind yourself that God doesn't give us that fear, and that He will be your strength and calm.

Prayer: Lord, in the midst of my fear, remind me of Your strength. Fill me with Your peace, and keep me calm.

Passing It On

But God composed the body, having given greater honor to that part which lacks it, that there should be no schism in the body, but that the members should have the same care for one another. And if one member suffers, all the members suffer with it; or if one member is honored, all the members rejoice with it.

—1 Corinthians 12:24–26

Every mother of a child with special needs hurts at some time. It is during those times that we need the comfort and help of God and His people. At other times, we feel God's strength and are gifted with the ability to cope. It is during those times that we can pass on the blessings that we have received.

When Jacob was transported from the hospital in which he was born to another hospital several miles away for diagnosis and treatment of his birth defect, he was given a little companion to share the ride. His mother found it in his crib the next day. As she lifted the little teddy bear from the crib, the mother was approached by a nurse who asked if the mother wanted to hear the story of the bear. Nodding, the mother turned to listen.

The nurse explained that there was a little boy born some distance away from the hospital who had been transported there by ambulance. His parents had tucked a little teddy bear in with him for the journey. They prayed that the little bear would represent the presence of God with their child. The little boy did not survive his trip. His grieving parents arrived at the hospital only to begin funeral arrangements.

As they gathered up their son's belongings, they handed over the bear to the ambulance driver with the request that it be given to the next baby that had to be transported. They wanted the next parents to know that God was there, even in the midst of sorrow. Jacob was the next baby transported.

When Jacob was well enough to leave the hospital, the bear went with him. It was placed on a shelf high above his bed. His mother looked at it each day, reminded of the loving sacrifice of those other parents and the steady presence of God.

Just after Jacob's fourth birthday, his mother's cousin, who lives on the other side of the country, gave birth to a daughter. Hannah was born missing almost half of her heart. She was stabilized and surgery was scheduled, the first of many she would have to endure. Jacob's mother prayed for Hannah and put together a little box of gifts and a Bible to send to Hannah.

She wrote a little note and mailed the box. She returned home from the post office smiling, for in the box was the little teddy bear and the story of two little boys as a reminder of God's presence.

Prayer: Lord, help me to see Your steadfast presence in my life and the life of my child. And, once I am able to see, help me to teach others to see also.

Excuses for Sin?

And the tongue is a fire, a world of iniquity. The tongue is so set among our members that it defiles the whole body, and sets on fire the course of nature; and it is set on fire by hell.

—James 3:6

We all fall. We all make mistakes. Every one of us has those moments when we succumb to the stress and anguish of our situation and lash out at those around us. We speak words that we know should never have been spoken. We wound those around us out of our pain. Sometimes we just want someone else to hurt as we do. Sometimes we just cannot handle one more glib statement. Sometimes we are so tired, we allow our own sinful nature to take control of our tongue.

But no matter the difficulties we face, sinful behavior has no excuse. We can see that our words hit their mark in the pained expression in our spouses' eyes. We feel that twinge of guilt when our children grow silent and hang their heads. We know the hurt of our friends when they back away.

What can we do when we lash out?

First of all we must confess that sin to God—with no excuses. He knows we are tired and stressed and hurting. But He also gives us the strength to avoid sinning if we are relying on Him. Ask God's forgiveness first.

Then we must go to those we have wounded. We must ask their forgiveness for our actions or words against them. And if they tell us it is all right, that they understand the struggle we are in, we need to let them know that it is *not* all right to hurt someone else, no matter what we are facing.

Once we receive forgiveness from God and the people we have sinned against, we must forgive ourselves. Self-contempt over sin is, in itself, sinful. Guilt over sin is justified and healthy, but continued self-contempt over a forgiven sin is a tool of evil.

We can brainstorm ways in which to control our tongue. Pray daily for God to control it, read the Word, fill your mind with the things of God. Talk to a counselor or pastor who may help you find ways to deal with the stress involved in raising your special child. Write your feelings and frustrations out in a journal. Take some time each day to treat yourself to something nice: a bath, a walk, a phone call to a friend.

Surrender your thoughts and your words to God, and watch Him help you control them.

Prayer: Lord, there are times that I sin against others with my tongue. I feel frustrated and stressed and allow myself to indulge in sin. I surrender my thoughts and words to You. Keep them pure, and never allow them to hurt others.

Sounds of Joy

Is anyone cheerful? Let him sing psalms.
—James 5:13

Joey was born with cerebral palsy. He was the second son, and the second with cerebral palsy. His mother was already taxed to her limits of strength and after much heart-wrenching deliberation, chose to give Joey up for adoption.

Ellen and Ray, having raised six children of their own, welcomed Joey into their lives. He arrived unable to communicate or control his body. Surgeries enabled him to sit up in a wheelchair. Extensive therapy and a letter board helped him to painstakingly spell out words to communicate. Eventually, Joey received a computer with a special keyboard that allowed him to play chess, write, and enter school.

Joey spent much of his time alone in the house, his parents being older and less able to transport him as he grew. The highlight of Joey's days were visits from his nieces and nephews, especially Ray-Ray.

Joey loved Ray-Ray, and that love was returned equally. When Ray-Ray would enter the room, Joey would erupt in squeals of joy, pounding the tray on his wheelchair, almost tipping himself to the floor. Ray-Ray would give him a high five and ask him how he was doing. Joey would grin and squeal again.

The two of them would spend long hours together as Ray-Ray taught Joey to read aloud. Ray-Ray would gently help him with words, repeating pronunciations over and over until Joey's garbled speech resembled the desired sounds. Then the pair would switch to chess, a game at which Joey grew quite adept. The house thundered with Joey's squeals the day he finally beat Ray-Ray!

Joey is middle-aged now, but his squeals of joy are still a delight to hear. Ray-Ray (now called simply Ray) not surprisingly became a teacher and opens the lives of hundreds of children to the joy of discovery. His students bask in the luxury of Ray-Ray's undivided attention.

Joey, unashamed, allowed his happiness to overflow into any room in which he sat. May we be as free with our happiness as this wonderful young man.

Prayer: Lord, help me to "sing" praise when I am happy. Let me show it to others who may, in turn, be helped in their own mood or situation.

Encourage the Disabled

> *But I would strengthen you with my mouth,*
> *And the comfort of my lips would relieve your grief.*
> —Job 16:5

Jaimie has a learning disability. She is an intelligent, beautiful, vivacious young lady who has many gifts. She sang in her high school choir, she played various sports, she had a circle of good friends who enjoyed her company. But she could not read like other people.

Jaimie spent part of her school day in a separate room working with a Learning Disabilities (LD) specialist. Jaimie attended several regular classes but took her tests in the LD room because the instructor had to read the questions to her. Then Jaimie would painstakingly write out her answers. Other times she would answer orally and the teacher would write it down for her. Essay tests were the most difficult for Jaimie.

She spent hours each night studying with her mother and her friends. She memorized facts and stories. She listened to books on tape. And she dreamed of going on to school after she graduated.

Jaimie worked hard, earning good grades. When the top ten students were announced for honors at graduation in May, Jaimie's name was on the list. There was immediate reaction by those ignorant of her disability. Accusations flew. Some thought Jaimie's grades were good only because she got "special help." Others thought she didn't take her tests at all. The school board reviewed the situation and announced its findings: Jaimie deserved her rank in the class and would graduate with honors.

Jaimie's friends and teachers stood by her, encouraging her through this difficult time, continually telling her to hold on to her dreams and desires. Jaimie continued to prove that her disability was not going to hold her back.

And she proved it all over again, graduating first from high school, and then from an institution of higher learning. She currently works as a sign language interpreter, a career that does not tax her reading skills but provides a vital service. Jaimie volunteers as an interpreter for services at her church.

She is still in touch with many of those who encouraged her through her high school struggles. Jaimie has told them that she never would have made it without their kind words.

Don't underestimate how much power our words carry for others . . . even our own little ones. Use your words wisely and look for ways to encourage all people, especially those who, like our children, have much to overcome.

Prayer: Lord, help me to always remember the impact my

words can have on another person. Help me to be one to encourage, not to tear down.

Protected

> *He shall cover you with His feathers,*
> *And under His wings you shall take refuge.*
> —Psalm 91:4

During my early teen years my family lived on a ten-acre hobby farm. We had a couple of dogs, many cats, goats, a lamb, dogs, ducks, and chickens. My chore each day was to feed the chickens and gather eggs. I loved to enter the henhouse and shoo away the biddies, collecting the warm eggs from the nests.

Sometimes, we would allow one of the hens to keep a clutch of eggs so that she could raise her babies. I loved the little yellow puff balls that would follow their mom around the yard. They would peep and scratch and peck at the ground. Their mother would scratch and peck beside them, seemingly unconcerned about their whereabouts.

One day I was throwing handfuls of corn for the chickens, watching the little ones scatter this way and that to find the yellow kernels. I noticed a nearby cat go suddenly still, her ears pointed toward some bushes. I heard the bush directly in front of me rustle. A black head poked out, beady black eyes searching the area. As it emerged a bit farther, I recognized the white stripe on the top of its head. I began to back slowly away—I sure didn't want to tangle with a skunk!

At almost the same moment, the chickens noticed the skunk. All the hens ran squawking to the henhouse. All of them but one. The mother hen began clucking urgently, calling her babies to her. They came without hesitation, gathering close to her feet. As I watched in amazement, she puffed out her feathers and lowered herself over her brood. She completely covered the babies. I couldn't see a single yellow feather nor a single little foot. The chicks had found refuge under the wings and feathers of the hen. The skunk, probably disappointed at finding no chicks in the yard, turned aside and waddled away.

In our times of trouble, God will cover us as completely as that hen hid her chicks. He promises to cover us and give us refuge. Just as the chicks ran to their mother, we need to run to Him. We need to gather at His feet and trust Him to gather us in.

Prayer: Lord, You are my refuge. Just as the hen protects and covers her chicks, so will You protect and cover those who seek safety in You. Thank You for this promise. Help me to run to You when I am troubled.

God Doesn't Make Mistakes

I will praise You, for I am fearfully and wonderfully made;
Marvelous are Your works,
And that my soul knows very well.

—Psalm 139:14

Your child may not be like a lot of other children. This little one in your care may have problems that many children will never face. You will have struggles and changes in your life that other mothers never dreamed of. Your road is different from what you may have expected in life.

But because your road is different doesn't mean it is a mistake. God doesn't go about creating life and then slapping a hand to His forehead when something doesn't turn out right. He isn't sitting on His heavenly throne saying, "Oh dear, now what should I do? That baby didn't turn out the way I had planned." There is no panic in the heavenly realm over your child.

Rather, God is looking with loving eyes at your baby and seeing the awesome and wonderful creation He has given you to raise. He knows that there are challenges ahead for both of you that others will not face. Each person has his or her own unique set of circumstances and struggles. Your road is different, but it is the road marked out just for you to travel. No one else is capable of it. He gave it to you. And each step of that road is full of opportunities and blessings along with the hardships of this life.

When He looks at you and your little one, the Lord doesn't see a damaged child or an unworthy mother. He sees beauty and light and love. He sees hearts that He created to love. He sees a mother entrusted with His precious creation—the only mother who is just right for this special child.

If anything, God is sitting on His throne and smiling in joy over the pairing of you and this wondrous baby. At the same time, He is promising you His love and aid throughout your special journey.

Your baby is no mistake. Your baby's challenges are not unfortunate occurrences over which God is wringing His hands. There is no catastrophe here. No, He is excited about the future for the two of you. He knows that mighty things can and will happen through you and through the life of your child if you allow Him to work.

Go ahead and grieve the dream you lost. But then turn your eyes to the adventure that God has set before you. See the baby that He fearfully and wonderfully made just for you to raise. Look with awe upon the unfolding of His mighty plan for your life.

Prayer: Lord, it is comforting to know that You don't make mistakes. I know that You have Your hand over me and my child. You have a plan for us.

A Cheerful Heart

A merry heart does good, like medicine,
But a broken spirit dries the bones.
—Proverbs 17:22

The nurse who was admitting a baby with Down's syndrome was surprised by the woman to whom she spoke. The baby was nine months old and was checking into the hospital to have a heart defect repaired. Many mothers would be frantic with worry, perhaps bemoaning their child's state.

But not this mother. She answered the questions on the forms calmly while she nursed her baby. After the nurse finished, the mother looked up with earnest eyes and told the nurse how thankful she was that the baby could breast-feed.

"She isn't too weak. Her tongue isn't too large. This surgery will only help to make her stronger!"

Of course, this mother understood the risks presented in heart surgery, but she chose to focus on the blessing of being able to nurse her baby. She never mentioned anything negative—no mention of the things her baby would not be able to do in life. She only spoke with thankfulness of those things that her baby could do.

At times, it can be so difficult to find the wonderful achievements of our special children. There can be so many negative issues that continually come to our attention.

Modern psychology—both secular and Christian—has taught us the health value of focusing on the "positives" in life. Focusing on the negative can cause depression, anxiety, anger, and bitterness—all traits that we know will harm us in the long run.

Have you taken the time to list the positive traits and achievements of your child? If you haven't, do so now. As others come to mind later, add them to your list. And when you find yourself dwelling on the negative, pull out your list and remind yourself of the blessings.

Prayer: Lord, thank You for the wonder that is my child. Keep my eyes focused on the blessings rather than the problems in raising this little one.

Love's Language

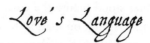

And when this sound occurred, the multitude came together, and were confused, because everyone heard them speak in his own language. Then they were all amazed and marveled, saying to one another, "Look, are not all these who speak Galileans? And how is it that we hear, each in our own language in which we were born?"

—Acts 2:6–8

Louis was a four-year-old boy with Down's syndrome. He was in the hospital because his tongue was so enlarged it obstructed his airway. Louis was afraid of the strange place, and he was frightened because he struggled to breathe. And he was also frightened because he only spoke Spanish and everyone on staff spoke English.

But Louis knew one song in English: "Old MacDonald." His nurse discovered this one afternoon while she bathed him. From that day on, that was what the nurse—and Louis—sang no matter what they were doing.

"Old MacDonald" rang out in the intensive care unit as Louis had his bath or was fed. The melody grew louder as his tracheostomy tube was changed or cleaned. Sometimes Louis was able to join in. Sometimes he couldn't. But his nurse sang.

It made Louis smile. And it made the scary things less threatening.

The nurse didn't have training in Spanish. She wasn't an interpreter. But she was speaking to Louis in a language he clearly understood: the language of love.

Just as when Peter stood before the crowds and spoke in a tongue everyone understood, no matter the native tongue, we can speak the universal language of love and compassion. We are enabled by the same Spirit that spoke through Peter on pentecost.

Use this language to speak to your child . . . your spouse . . . your family . . . yourself. Reach out to a new mother struggling to adjust to a special-needs child. What you say is really not as important as the love behind it.

Let the God who is love pour love into your heart and through your life to others. Allow Him to open your eyes to those speaking that same love to you through their actions and their presence in your life.

Prayer: Lord, help me to see the love You send to me through others. Help me to understand the language of love in daily actions and concerns. Use me to speak Your love to those who need to hear it.

Encouraging the Discouraged

*Fathers, do not provoke your children,
lest they become discouraged.*
—Colossians 3:21

Pericles was born without a diaphragm. His lungs were compressed by his liver and intestines. His first days were spent on a bypass machine as doctors slowly reconstructed his insides. As a result, his development was seriously delayed. He couldn't even speak.

Pericles had a special blessing. He had a family who was devoted to him, but, more important, he had a mother who believed in him.

His mother was with him each day in the hospital, learning sign language right along with her son. She learned to clean the instruments that kept her son alive. And she told her son of the great things he would do one day.

She told him that he could grow up to be anything he wanted. She told him that he could take over and run his daddy's business. She told him of the schools he could attend that had wonderful programs for children like him. She told him that, God willing, and with a little more time than some children required, he could achieve his dreams. She told him God had great things in store for him.

William, on the other hand, had a disability that delayed speech and required surgery as well. However, his father would not accept his son's differences. The father refused to name the problem, let alone work with William to improve his skills. William never practiced his speech therapy with his father. He never felt the compassion and belief of the most important man in his life.

Within the first two years of William's life, his father stopped attending church, bitter over the problems his son endured.

Which child do you think grew up to be successful in life, faith-filled, and confident?

Prayer: Lord, help me to be an encouragement to my child. Help me to see the great things You have in store for this precious child. Help me to encourage my child to be all that You designed this little one to be.

Everything in Common

Now all who believed were together,
and had all things in common.
                        —Acts 2:44

The waiting room at the clinic was filled with children and their parents. The children played in the corner with various toys and blocks. The parents watched with smiles. The wait to see the team of doctors was long; often a number of hours would pass before each family saw all the doctors and could return home.

During this time, friendships were begun. Some were renewed. The parents relaxed in the peace of knowing they wouldn't have to explain their child's problems to a shocked audience. Every child there was disfigured. Their voices were nasal or distorted, their words garbled or slurred.

None of the older children hid their scars, knowing they were totally accepted just as they were. The parents chatted softly about the hardships of raising their children in the public eye. They spoke painfully of the taunting and stares their children endured.

But there was none of that here. Each child was free simply to be a child. No one stared or made them feel self-conscious. They shared toys and games, soon asking their parents for snacks to share with their new friends.

Glancing around the room, I saw mothers reading to children they didn't even know. A father cut strips of apple for a small group of children. One mother reached over to steady a toddler who belonged to someone else. An older child with a scarred face rocked a little one who would grow up with a matching set of scars.

The room had become a community, each parent having two things in common with the others. Each had a child with a disfiguring condition, and each fiercely loved that child, wanting to help and protect him. The children simply knew that, in this room, they were not "different," but accepted.

What a beautiful example of fellowship. We, as believers, should reflect this type of acceptance in our own lives. Every person has scars, whether they are physical or emotional. And those scars may make them hesitant to come into community with others. Because of our unique experience with our children, we can be the hand that reaches out in acceptance and love to others.

Prayer: Lord, help me to be the one who reaches out to others in love and acceptance. Help me to see each person with Your eyes of compassion.

Simple Joy

Let everything that has breath praise the LORD.
—Psalm 150:6

Brecken faces a lifetime of physical problems. At the age of six, he has already endured years of therapies and surgery. He has vision and hearing problems. His speech is extremely nasal and high-pitched—most people cannot understand him. He lives in constant pain.

But Brecken is one of the most joy-filled people I have ever met. He literally dances with joy when he meets someone new. His eyes sparkle and a huge, lopsided grin lights up his little face. Invariably, Brecken will grasp his new friend's hand (everyone is a friend to Brecken) and pull him off to explore some new and amazing thing he has discovered.

When Brecken's mother gives him a cookie, Brecken immediately breaks it into pieces to be shared with anyone in the room. He will often give away the entire cookie, saving none for himself. He beams as he watches his friends enjoy his cookie.

Although it is difficult, Brecken enjoys racing across the yard with his buddies. He trots along behind them, shouting encouragement and cheering the winner . . . which he never is himself. He plays kick-ball and never reaches first base without some help in the form of purposely missed or overthrown balls on the part of the opposing team. He has never scored a run himself, but he cheers loudest when the others do.

Brecken is bursting with joy. He overflows with it from the moment he springs out of bed in the morning to the instant he closes his eyes in sleep at night.

The only time Brecken is sad is when he goes to the hospital for his checkups or other procedures. But he is not sad over his own troubles. He grieves over the pain he sees in the faces of other children. Often he will approach a frightened child, pat them on the shoulder, and whisper encouragement.

Brecken was asked once why he was so happy when he had so much pain.

"'Cuz God loves me!" came his simple reply.

Prayer: Lord, You have filled our lives with so much to be enjoyed. Help us to take the time to enjoy what we can, trusting You to take care of what struggles we face. And along the way, help us to encourage others who are hurting.

Tough Love

For they [human fathers] indeed for a few days chastened us as seemed best to them, but He for our profit, that we may be partakers of His holiness. Now no chastening seems to be joyful for the present, but painful; nevertheless, afterward it yields the peaceable fruit of righteousness to those who have been trained by it.

—Hebrews 12:10–11

It was my decision to put my son through this pain. The thought struck me as I rocked my child. He clung to me, whimpering, his brow furrowed in pain. It had been only a few hours since Aiden's surgery, and he was not a happy boy. I was not a happy mother.

I knew that this surgery was to benefit him. He would speak more clearly. He would be able to eat without residual food dripping from his nostrils. The surgery would complete the roof of his mouth, allowing him to function more naturally. He might even be able to blow out the candles on his next birthday cake!

There was so much good that would come from this surgery. So, after weighing the pain against the benefits, I had agreed to the procedure.

That is not to say I did not weep for my child. I did. I cuddled him and sang to him as tears coursed my cheeks. I hated to see him in pain. My heart ached in a way that it never had before. He looked at me with tear-filled blue eyes, and I was awash with guilt, knowing I made the decision to put him here.

But the guilt was not so strong that I would not agree to future surgeries, because I knew Aiden would truly be better off because of the short time of pain. So I cuddled him and comforted him as he went through this difficult time, trying to help him in any way I could.

I cannot help but think of how much more deeply the Lord feels our pain when that is what He must give us to help us become all He desires us to be. He has our ultimate good in mind but knows that sometimes we must endure pain in order to grow and improve.

At the same time, He aches for our pain, necessary though it may be. He weeps with us and longs to comfort us, reaching out His strong arms to embrace us.

During these times, rather than becoming angry and bitter, we must seek Him and His plan for our lives, enduring the present pain in order to reach a higher level of righteousness and peace.

Remember that in any trial His love and compassion accompany us.

Prayer: Lord, thank You for Your watchful eye and Your knowledge of what is best for our lives. Help me to stay focused on Your ultimate plan, knowing that all You do is for my ultimate benefit.

Ministering Angels

For He shall give His angels charge over you,
To keep you in all your ways.
            —Psalm 91:11

I firmly believe that my home is filled with angels. God's Word tells me that angels have been sent to guard and protect me and my family. I am just as positive that there are angels watching over you.

But I don't believe that these angels are the only ones God has sent.

Mary spent her life as a pediatric nurse. She loved and cared for the little ones who passed through her life. Later she nursed her husband through terminal cancer. Finding her life lonely, she continued reaching out to others. She spent her spare time visiting homes to help young mothers or those with special-needs children. She quietly used her wealth to set up funds to help those whose income or insurance did not cover their medical needs. She volunteered her time without complaint or boasting.

No menial task was too much for Mary. She spent years caring for twins born to Russian immigrants. She never received money from the family, but she was rewarded with the love of two beautiful children. Mary cared for a girl with leukemia without thought to her own needs.

This woman had lived a life of hard work and had nursed her husband through his dying days. She could be enjoying her retirement without a thought of the plight of others. But she spends her days acting as God's hands in a hurting world.

Look around you. God has sent tangible help—"angels" on earth—to stand beside you. They may be in the form of doctors and nurses, or your family or friends. They may be the smiling woman who greets you in a store, or the man who helps you lift a burden for a moment. They may be the cheerful voice of the disc jockey on your local Christian radio station, or the acquaintance who calls to see how you are doing.

Each of these people is really God's voice saying, "I am here. You are not alone. I will always be here. I love you, and I will help you. Come to Me with your struggles."

Prayer: Lord, thank You for Your angels who guard and protect us. And thank You for the "angels on earth," the people You send into my life to help remind me of Your love and concern.

The Terror of Night

You shall not be afraid of the terror by night.
—Psalm 91:5

Alex woke up at three o'clock in the morning, crying in pain. His parents grabbed their three-year-old son and rushed him to the hospital. Within moments he was torn, screaming, from his mother's arms and taken into surgery.

It was discovered that Alex had a congenital defect that caused his intestines to become completely blocked. Alex was a very sick little boy. His doctor found only two other documented cases like his in medical journals.

For days after the surgery, Alex refused to eat or drink. He lay in bed holding his mother's hand, screaming in terror if she moved out of his sight. The pastor of the church Alex attended visited him in the hospital, praying over him and telling him that Jesus was also there to take care of him, just like Mommy.

Little by little, Alex began to heal physically. But his fear of being taken from his mother remained for years. He would sneak out of his bed at night to curl up on the floor beside his mother's bed.

One day in Sunday school, the teacher explained to Alex that he is never, ever alone, that Jesus is beside him every moment. And, what's more, that God has surrounded him with angels. They read Psalm 91 together. Alex looked up with shining eyes and said, "You mean, God will always be with me? I don't ever have to be afraid to be alone ever again?"

His teacher smiled. "God is always with you. You never have to be afraid of being alone again."

Suddenly, Alex was sleeping through the night in his own bed. His nightmares stopped. He trotted off to school with a quick wave to his mother, no longer clinging to her in fear.

Are you afraid? When darkness comes, do you worry about your child, your finances, your life? Place these terrors of the night into the hands of God. Let Him bring you the peace that comes in knowing God is in control—you don't have to be afraid ever again.

Prayer: Lord, today I give You my private fears. I place them in Your hands, knowing You are big enough to handle anything. You are in control. I need not fear.

Rain in the Springtime

Ask the LORD for rain
In the time of the latter rain.
—Zechariah 10:1

I love the spring. It is by far my favorite season. It is fresh and damp and smells so clean after the stale air of the long winter. Windows are flung open, and the newness of spring air rushes through the house. The rains come and wash away the slushy winter residue. The brown, dry grass transforms into lush, green lawns. Yellow dandelions pop sunshine faces skyward. Everything is refreshed and new.

When the first scent of spring wafts through the air, I become almost giddy. I just can't be depressed in the spring. I feel just as refreshed and new as the world around me.

I feel the same way after spending focused time with God. After the long, stale times of struggle and pain, I can turn to Him for my own personal springtime. Time spent reading the Bible, listening to a sermon, attending a retreat, or in extended prayer is like flinging the windows open and allowing the newness of spring air to rush through my soul.

The cleansing rain of the Spirit washes away the slushy residue of days spent in worry and strife or apathy. The brown dryness of my soul changes once again to lush green. My own sunshine face once again turns skyward toward the God who renews me. Everything is refreshed and new.

Are you in that long winter? Do you feel dry and brown, stale and slushy? Are you ready for the cleansing scent of spring to lighten your soul? Ask the Lord for rain in the springtime to cleanse your soul of winter and refresh you.

Attend a retreat. Find respite from your daily trials. Ask someone to tend your child while you go on a long walk or drive, then spend that time talking to God. Read the Bible. Spend time reading passages about God's love for you. Revisit the story of Jesus' time on this planet. Attend church services and let the Spirit of God move through you.

You will come away from these times refreshed and new, breathing the heady scent of God's springtime in your soul.

Prayer: Lord, the seasons remind me of the renewal You offer each of us. Allow me today to spend time walking in the rain that can cleanse and renew my spirit.

Finding Rest

Come to Me, all you who labor and are heavy laden, and I will give you rest.

—Matthew 11:28

Lori's son has attention deficit disorder (ADD). He cannot stay focused on an activity for more than a moment or two. He is constantly in motion unless he is asleep. Often he is in trouble at school for disrupting class. Lori cannot remember ever being in a public place when her son did not draw disapproving glares—glares that soon turned her way.

Lori worked with doctors, counselors, and teachers to help her son compensate for his disorder. She battled daily at home to teach her son how to control his behavior. Often the two of them would end the day exhausted and in tears.

Lori's friends began to avoid her, not understanding that ADD is as real as any other disorder or disability. It is not caused by a lack of discipline—stricter discipline will never "cure" Lori's son. But when Lori tries to explain this to her friends and neighbors, she sees the resistance in their eyes.

She has begun retreating into seclusion. If she and her son remain at home, Lori doesn't have to face the accusing stares that say she is a bad mother. She doesn't hear the whispers that say she should give her son a "good spanking" to control his behavior.

Lori has stopped asking others for help with her son. Baby-sitters don't come to the house anymore. They say her boy is a "brat." The neighbor children don't come to the yard. Their parents say they don't have to play with her boy because Lori doesn't discipline him.

Lori is lonely and exhausted, wondering where to turn.

She needs only to hear the gentle voice of the Savior calling out, "Come to Me." He promises her rest and help with her burdens. He will be there for her when others turn away. He will be there when others accuse her or voice their disapproval. He will be there when she is tired of the daily struggle. He will lift her chin, wipe her eyes, and give her strength to continue.

Prayer: Lord, You are the Source of rest and strength. Thank You for lifting my burdens.

Held in Loving Arms

His left hand is under my head,
And his right hand embraces me.
—Song of Solomon 2:6

It melts the heart to see a baby toddle to her parent and lift her arms straight up in a gesture of love and trust, asking to be held. A baby feels safest in the arms of a loving parent. They often will run to those arms when strange situations and people confront them. Once in the safety of those arms, they can observe the new person calmly without fear. After a few moments the child will wiggle to get back down, secure and comforted, and continue walking forward.

Those arms represent security, safety, comfort, and love. They reach out and gather in a child when she is hurt or afraid. They hug her when a new task is accomplished. They lift her when the task before her is too big or too difficult to accomplish alone. They rock her to sleep at the end of the day.

How many of us look back at the trusting time of childhood, wishing we could be back in that time when we had someone older and wiser to gather us into their arms and make the difficulties manageable?

Did you know that you are in a time and place in which someone older and wiser is waiting to gather you in?

Your heavenly Father is with you, eager to wrap His loving arms around you and lift you up. He longs to comfort your pain and ease your fears. He rejoices with you when new tasks are accomplished—by you or your child. He waits to lift you when the tasks ahead seem too difficult to accomplish alone. He will rock you asleep at the end of the day.

Turn to Him. He is our *Abba*, the term that finds its English equivalent in the word *Daddy*. Just as you wrap your arms around your precious special child, allow your Daddy—the Lord of heaven and earth—to wrap His arms around you.

Prayer: Lord, I come to You today to sit in Your lap as Your precious child. Hold me today, for just a little while, until I am ready to once again walk forward.

Good Times

When times are good, be happy.
—Ecclesiastes 7:14 NIV

Darcy is seven years old. She has spina bifida. Her condition is such that she is on a ventilator and cannot move anything but her head. Her parents love her and care for her tenderly.

Periodically, Darcy enters the hospital for a "tune-up," what her parents call respite care: a time for them to rest and recharge their energy as a couple. Darcy doesn't mind. She knows that everyone needs a bit of a break sometimes.

Shortly after Darcy's seventh birthday, her parents planned an adults-only trip to Florida. Darcy's brothers stayed with friends, and Darcy came to the hospital to visit the nurses she had come to know so well over the years.

After Darcy was settled into her bed, her aunt arrived, her arms loaded with bulging paper bags. She called out a cheery greeting to Darcy and told her that there was no reason she couldn't enjoy her own Florida vacation! Briskly she emptied the paper bags and began decorating the hospital room with streamers, paper palm trees, and construction paper fish. Within minutes the room was transformed into a tropical paradise. Darcy giggled at the astonished looks of the nurses who entered "Florida" to take her vitals or check her ventilator.

Her aunt made a memory for Darcy that will stay with her forever. When times are difficult or she is unhappy, she can think back on her "Florida" vacation at the hospital.

Darcy's time in respite care could have been dull and depressing. But her aunt chose to seize those days and make them into good times.

Raising a child with special needs is not easy. Some days are hard and sad. But there will be times here and there, even in the worst of conditions, that can be happy moments. We need to hold those precious moments to our hearts and minds, allowing God's love to shine through. It doesn't have to take a decorated hospital room to bring a smile to your child's face— or to yours. Just keep your eyes open for those happy moments.

You'll discover that the more you look for them, the more you will find.

Prayer: Lord, help me to see each happy moment scattered throughout my life as a sign of Your love for me and my child.

Finding Ways to Play

The spirit of a man will sustain him in sickness.

—Proverbs 18:14

A five-year-old boy had suffered a terrifying accident. He had touched an electrical transformer box that had been inadvertently left unlocked. Blessed to be alive, he had lost both his arms at just above the elbow due to electric burns.

Once he was feeling better physically, he was bewildered and listless. His family was angry and worried about their child. He wanted to go back to the life he had led before the accident, but that just was not possible.

Slowly he came to realize that he couldn't play Nintendo or color, two of his favorite pastimes. After several days, he grew bored with watching videos. He wanted—needed—to play.

His parents sat with him daily, trying to figure out how to help their little boy as he grew more restless and depressed. Finally the hospital's creative play coordinator brought in a box of Matchbox cars.

At first glance, those in the room believed that the small toys would be frustrating and useless to a little boy with no arms. However, they smiled as they realized that cars can be driven across the floor with a little boy's feet! Soon the nurses and family members were on the floor with the little boy, all barefoot and laughing. He got so adept at driving his cars that he didn't even mind that the nurses often cheated by using their hands.

The family watched their little boy blossom into the bright, sunny child he had been before the accident.

If we spend our days serious and worried, it affects our children. Get down on the floor or pull up a chair and find a new and unique way to play with your child. You will be amazed at the lift it gives you both.

Prayer: Lord, thank You for giving us creative minds. Help me to find ways to play with my child in new and fun ways.

Ever – Present Help   ❧

> *God is our refuge and strength,*
> *A very present help in trouble.*
> —Psalm 46:1

Kim is a pediatric nurse. She worked for years with the sickest patients at Children's Hospital in Milwaukee, Wisconsin. She left that job feeling gifted in having been a small comfort to the children and parents who had crossed her path. She wrote:

Where was God when we couldn't stabilize the post–open-heart kids; when we got the children with meningitis too late to treat; when the ventilators kept pushing air but the heart was too sick to keep beating; when the children were missing too many pieces to put back together; when the medicine wouldn't work?

I believe He was waiting with open arms to gather those children close. He was there to comfort grieving family and staff. He was there to keep hope alive.

Amen.

Prayer: Lord, help me keep hope alive.

Brothers in Adversity

A friend loves at all times,
And a brother is born for adversity.
　　　　　　—Proverbs 17:17

He was a big man-child, almost two hundred pounds, with Duchenne's dystrophy, a muscle-wasting disease. Although his muscles were failing, his mind was unaffected. He was eighteen years old when he was hospitalized to be put on a ventilator.

Several times he would panic on the ventilator and fight it, feeling as though he were suffocating. The best medicine for him were the daily visits by his brothers, ages sixteen and twenty.

Without fail for over a month, the two brothers came to the hospital to help him get out of bed and into a chair. They would patiently feed him his dinner, laughing and chatting all the while. There was a lot of kidding and "guy" talk.

I am sure those two young men had many things they could have been doing: high school or college activities, dating, or hanging out with friends. But they spent their time with their disabled brother when he truly needed them.

I am also sure that if someone told them they were admired for their dedication to their brother, they would pause, confused, and say that they were *brothers*—that's what any brother would do!

Do you have family who are standing by you and your child? Or are you that person for your little one? Perhaps there are Christian brothers and sisters who stand in that place in your life. Indeed, if this is the case, you are then blessed with precious relationships.

Allow those people to love you and help you along the way. Find comfort in their care.

Prayer: Lord, You have made us to be in relationship first with You, and then with others. Thank You for those You have placed in my life.

Carry Each Other's Burdens

Bear one another's burdens, and so fulfill the law of Christ.
—Galatians 6:2

Leigh was overwhelmed when her baby was born with a heart defect. Although not strong herself, she moved into the cramped hospital room to be with her baby. She tried hard not to get in the way of the nurses who cared for her little one. Feeling unsure and exhausted, she finally succumbed to tears.

Seeing her, one of the nurses approached and touched her hand gently. Looking up, Leigh saw tears coursing down the cheeks of the nurse. The woman embraced her, and Leigh felt strengthened by the compassion in those tears.

A late-night phone call roused B. J. It was a hospital in a neighboring town. A baby had just been born with the same rare condition as her child. Could she come and talk to the mother? B. J. grabbed some photographs of her child and rushed out the door.

Gently knocking on the door, B. J. heard a strangled voice call her in. Sitting in the bed was a weeping woman. B. J.

didn't speak a word, she simply moved to the woman, wrapped her arms around her and wept with her. There would be time to look at the pictures later.

We are in a truly unique situation. As parents of children with special needs, we know, as no one else can, the confusion and pain a new mother feels when her baby is born with differences.

Let other people help out with the meals or the laundry. Let a friend baby-sit for older siblings or clean the house. Let a neighbor mow the lawn or shovel the snow. Our ministry is in letting this new mother know she is not alone. We can help lift one of the heaviest burdens that a new mother carries.

If you are that new mother, please know you are not alone. If one of us has not found you, seek us out. Call a local Bible church and ask to be connected with another mother like you. We are here, ready to help you in any way the Lord would have us do so.

Prayer: Lord, You have put us on this earth to help one another. Just as others throughout history have helped carry the burdens of their neighbors, help me to lighten someone else's load.

Bearing Up

> *For it is commendable if a man bears up under the pain of unjust suffering because he is conscious of God.*
>
> —1 Peter 2:19 NIV

Jan lived a hard life. She was a mother to not one, but two children with mental disabilities. Tim was so severely impaired that he never learned to speak or use his hands or feet. He died at the age of nineteen. Lois had a milder impairment and outlived her mother. Jan raised three other sons, all of whom became pastors later in life. One son had turned to drugs and alcohol to drown his feelings over his brother and sister before finally finding the love and compassion of Christ. He went on to pastor one of the largest churches in his area.

At the age of sixty-three Jan was diagnosed with the cancer that eventually killed her. She could have lamented the difficult life she had led, the pain of losing her son, the struggle to raise two disabled children, the irony of getting cancer just when life seemed to be sailing along smoothly. But she did not complain. She became mother to the entire church. Everyone called her "Ma." She tirelessly spent her time caring not only for her daughter and her aging mother, but for any woman in the church body who had a crisis at home.

Ma became the head of the prayer chain, personally calling the people she prayed for to see how they were doing. She organized meals to be sent to the houses, or women to come in and clean. She spent hours daily caring for anyone who needed her.

Each of Ma's acts of service was like a sweet, sun-drenched dandelion. The dandelion is a little flower that is often overlooked and trod upon. It quietly springs up and holds fast. And when we take the time to look closely, we can see that the dandelion is a beautiful flower with laced petals and a fresh scent. An entire field of them is a glorious drenching of bright yellow.

Ma's life was spent scattering dandelions until the field was

full. Little seeds flew outward on feathered wings to scatter
and spread as others began emulating her life of service.

We all have the choice to spend our time lamenting our
lives, or we can be like Ma, using what we know to serve others
and God despite our suffering.

Will you follow the legacy of this humble servant and scatter
the seeds of service in your church and community? Before you
know it, each simple act will blossom until you have sown a field
that shines gloriously with the sunshine brightness of God.

Prayer: Lord, I want to be like Jan, scattering Your good
works throughout my neighborhood and church. Help me to
plant the dandelions of anonymous good works until there is
a shining yellow field before You.

Comfort

*And our hope for you is steadfast, because we know that as you are
partakers of the sufferings, so also you will partake of the consolation.*
—2 Corinthians 1:7

Some things are universal: People will suffer pain, whether
it be physical or emotional. God is faithful. We all need to love
and be loved. Babies should be rocked.

Kim, a pediatric nurse, insists that rocking a baby is as
important as medicine or medical procedures. "Every baby
needs to be rocked—the baby who was shaken so hard she
couldn't breathe on her own, the babies with Down's syndrome, the babies on ventilators or with tracheal malacia and
tracheostomies, the babies who were post–open-heart sur-

gery—all were comforted when rocked. Crying stopped, heart rate slowed, and they slept when rocked in a rocking chair. We had the chairs in every room in the hospital."

For almost a week after his third surgery Aiden could be calmed only in a rocking chair. He slept in my arms as the chair creaked back and forth, back and forth. The motion became his seduction into the painless sleep he needed in order to heal.

Lisa described this experience in the hospital after her son's first heart surgery:

> Liam would lay in the crib and moan, even when he was asleep. I would sing to him and hold his little hands, but it really didn't seem to do anything for him. Finally a nurse brought a rocking chair into the intensive care unit. She helped me get Liam . . . and all his tubes and monitors . . . into my lap on the chair. In just a few minutes, Liam was sleeping so soundly the moaning stopped. He turned his face against me and zonked out. From that day on, I rocked him every chance I got. The nurses said it was the reason he got well so soon.

Janet remembers her first visit to a Romanian orphanage. She sat on the floor surrounded by young, eager faces, many of whom were starved for her gentle touch. She rocked one small child on her lap. Glancing up, she saw another child, about age three, who wrapped his arms around himself and began to imitate her rocking motion.

Every baby needs to be rocked.

Prayer: Lord, in this sometimes difficult world, You have provided little comforts. Rocking is one that has no cost and can do so much. Help me to find the time to rock my child, even as You hold and comfort me.

Sparing the Rod

He who spares his rod hates his son,
But he who loves him disciplines him promptly.
—Proverbs 13:24

Children are very intuitive. They can pick up on their parents' weaknesses quickly. My son learned early that I was hesitant to make him cry after his surgeries. That meant he could get away with a lot in the first few months after returning home from the hospital. I justified my lack of action on the fact that he had just been through so much pain and tears that he needed a bit of a break.

The result was the emergence of a spoiled little boy who threw tantrums to get whatever he wanted. When his brothers and sisters began complaining about his behavior, I was forced to take a careful look at my own failure to discipline him.

I realized my real motivation was guilt over his surgeries. I hated being the one to decide his surgical schedule. I hated the fact that I chose to place him in these situations—even though I knew they were for his ultimate benefit. My heart would tear at each wail of pain, each slow tear and look of fear. I hate seeing him hurt! I realized that I could spare him the pain now only to have him suffer later in life with severe disfigurement and communicative disorders.

The decision was "pain now for future good."

I came to realize that my discipline methods needed to reflect that same policy. He could endure the pain of discipline, whether it was something simple such as a lack of privileges or something stronger such as a time-out or grounding, in order to have future benefits.

If I did not enforce the "pain now" in discipline, he would suffer later in life with severe personality and social problems.

I still hate seeing him cry, but I know that a few tears now as he learns self-control and acceptable behavior are worth the proper character development of my son. He is becoming a delightful little boy who loves to make others smile, help his daddy, and play with other children—with few tantrums!

Prayer: Thank You, Lord, that we can understand that discipline is for teaching and helping our children become the men and women of God You designed them to be. Help me to remain firm and fair while raising this child.

Joy and Grief

Even in laughter the heart may sorrow,
And the end of mirth may be grief.
—Proverbs 14:13

Have you ever noticed people pulling back in hesitation when you laugh over some silly thing your child has said or done? They would be laughing right along with you if your child did not have differences. But people aren't always comfortable laughing over the funny things our special children say and do.

Have you ever felt split into two people—one who is laughing and enjoying your little one while the other is aching and grieving over the struggles the two of you face? Have you ever tried to explain this to others only to have them shake their heads, unable to understand?

Take heart. All of those feelings and reactions are normal and even healthy. Our children do funny and precious things every day, and yet we may be hesitant to share them with others, a hesitation we would never have if our children did not have special needs.

Once I spoke to a large group at a midwestern university, sharing a funny story about each of my children—except Aiden. I was afraid they would think I was making fun of my child rather than enjoying him.

I also discovered that I grieved over the changes that resulted each time my child had surgery. After the first one, I missed Aiden's huge, double smile that was a result of his cleft. It took me months to get over losing it. When his palate was completed, he began speaking more clearly, and I began to miss the speech patterns he had developed to compensate for his disability.

I liked ducks that said "mack, mack" and pigs that said "moink, moink." I thought those words were precious and a unique part of Aiden. I am getting used to ducks that say "quack" and pigs that say "oink," but it will take some time.

At the same time I am eager to have my child speak like his friends, clearly and concisely. I work daily with him on his speech drills. I take him to language group once a week and to see Heidi, his beloved speech therapist.

Many mothers have expressed the same dichotomy. They fluctuate through joy and grief, laughter and tears, almost every day—sometimes many times a day. It is typical in the life of a woman raising a special-needs child. And God understands when you feel split this way. He laughs and cries with you.

Prayer: Life is never dull with my special child. Thank You, Lord, for the range of emotions You have given me so that I can cope with each day. I know that You understand even when others may not.

Responding to Pain

> *I have killed a man for wounding me,*
> *Even a young man for hurting me.*
> *If Cain shall be avenged sevenfold,*
> *Then Lamech seventy-sevenfold.*
> —Genesis 4:23–24

Five generations after Cain killed his brother Abel, Lamech was born. Lamech was the first man recorded in the Bible to marry more than one woman at a time. Lamech also seemed to look out for number one.

When he was hurt by a young man, Lamech felt justified in killing him. He even quoted God's promise to Cain and arrogantly increased it for himself. However, he missed a critical factor. God vowed to avenge Cain, while Lamech avenged himself.

How do you respond to pain? Do you retaliate or get revenge? Perhaps you retreat, isolating yourself to insulate yourself from pain while falling into the mire of self-pity. Others may regress into a state of regret (I wish I'd never . . .). Some run to find relief in anything that makes them feel better, whether it is drugs and alcohol, shopping, eating, or busyness.

Raising a child with differences will involve pain. Raising any child involves pain. We need to decide how we are going to respond to that pain.

We could try to seek revenge against those who may have a hand in our pain. It would be easy to strike out at those who tease your child or say volumes without even speaking. But what would that accomplish other than causing another person to feel pain, something God would never condone?

Self-pity is unhealthy. Isolating yourself in it is really an excuse to wallow, to not return to health. God wants us to feel our pain, not deny it. However, He doesn't want us to remain there as an emotional hostage. The same goes for continually second-guessing our choices. Sometimes it is too late to do anything more about them than to turn to God and rise above them.

When we run to something to find relief, it becomes our drug of choice, our god. We then dislodge the Lord from His rightful place in our lives.

We need to respond to pain by turning to the only One who can help us. He allows us time to weep and to grieve, and then He gently leads us forward to a place of healing and peace.

Do you need that touch from Him today? Take a moment to receive it, pouring your pain at His feet.

Prayer: Lord, sometimes the pain of living can seem unbearable. I know that I can find many ways to cope with that pain.

Today I choose to lay it at Your feet. Heal me and ease my pain and sorrow. I turn to You.

Denial and Self-Contempt

Woe to you, blind guides . . . Fools and blind!
—Matthew 23:16–17

Tom refused to look at his disabled child. He alternated between insisting that there was nothing wrong with the baby and insisting that there was nothing to be done about him. He refused to participate in discussions about his child's future. He didn't help his wife with the baby's care. He did not tell his coworkers that he had a child. When asked, he told one person the child had died at birth!

Tom was in denial for years. He moved from that denial to a strong contempt for his child, other children, himself, and God. Eventually, when his marriage began to fall apart, Tom found the one place where shame was put to death once and for all: the cross of Jesus Christ.

Denial can be a normal part of grieving in its early stages, often softening the shock we face. However, we cannot stay there. Have you seen signs of denial in your own life or that of your spouse? Denial can be seen in the following manifestations: excuse-making, making explanations that water down the seriousness of the situation, pretending there is nothing wrong, playing ignorant when faced with difficult decisions, lying to others or yourself, defensiveness, shifting blame, avoiding consequences, joking about the situation without addressing it, and ignoring it.

Be careful that your coping style doesn't shift from denial into a strong form of anger called contempt. Self-contempt may cause you to believe you are a failure and deserve the pain you live in, which will lead to serious problems. Contempt toward others may be evident when you hate the person who exposes your hidden coping styles. You may hate those who have caused you pain. You may even secretly hate the child you hold because of the pain and stress of your situation. Your anger may even pour forth into contempt for God.

Contempt is one way to deal with shame and anger. It is our way of punishing ourselves and others for the pain in our lives. We can become blinded by it.

Peter and Judas both reached times of denial and self-contempt. They both admitted they were wrong in their actions (Peter in denying Christ, Judas in betraying Him). They both knew Jesus was innocent. They both had regret and remorse over their actions.

Judas stopped there. He did not repent and turn to Jesus for forgiveness. He killed himself. Peter turned to Jesus—to Calvary and the cross, where shame is put to death so that we no longer need to punish ourselves. We can all experience the forgiveness and freedom Peter found there.

Prayer: Lord, help me to cope only by turning to You and those You send to help in Your stead. If I have fallen into self-contempt and denial, lead me to those who can help me either professionally or in the Church, with the ultimate destination being at the foot of the cross, in Your presence.

Don't Limit God

And he did what was right in the sight of the LORD.

—2 Kings 22:2

Josiah became king at the age of eight and reigned in Jerusalem until he was thirty-nine. After years of evil and decadence, Israel was finally brought back to a right standing with God during Josiah's reign.

Josiah had an unwavering dedication to God. He could have made excuses and limited God's work through his life. After all, he was incredibly young to be king. But he wasn't too young to give his life to serving God and His people. Paul echoed this many years later when he exhorted Timothy to not let anyone look down on him because of his age.

Josiah could have spent his life lamenting his background. It has been a trend in our nation for many years to blame our own choices and failings on our family of origin. Take a look at Josiah's family. His father, Amon, was extremely wicked, reigning for only two years before he was assassinated by his own officials. Amon worshiped idols and forgot about the God of Israel. Amon had followed in the steps of his own father, Manasseh, who had reigned for fifty-five years. Manasseh was the one who had reintroduced idolatry and the occult to Israel. He seduced God's people into doing more evil than the pagan nations around them!

Yet Josiah took responsibility for his own actions, walking with God and staying sensitive to the needs of God's people. He was willing to stand against the evil of the land. He had a steel backbone and a heart of warmth. He cleaned up the land and kept a right relationship with God despite his youth and shaky background.

Each one of us has a responsibility to base our actions and responses on God's Word rather than on our background or current situation, even when that situation may seem unfair or unjust. We need to develop that steel backbone when it comes to compromising our faith. But we need to have a tender and compassionate heart.

Don't let the current situation with your child or your anger over your circumstances sway you from a right relationship with the God who will sustain and love you.

Prayer: Lord, despite my current struggles and anything in my background that might keep me from seeking You, I commit myself to You today. Help me to remember Josiah, a boy who overcame a terrible background to become one of the greatest kings of Israel. If You can help that little boy, I know You can help me.

Walking with God

And Enoch walked with God.
—Genesis 5:24

Walking is one of the best forms of exercise. It is gentle on the joints, moves the body, and increases heart rate. It is recommended for cardiovascular fitness. Because of these recommendations, Lindsay began walking. At first she walked with her children in a stroller. Eventually, as her children grew older, she walked with her dog.

Late in life, Lindsay and her husband had another baby. Licia was born with severe Down's syndrome. Lindsay spent a long winter tending her child. Although she loved her daughter, she struggled with loneliness and depression.

When the spring thaw began, Lindsay's husband urged her to continue her walks. She resisted, claiming no one else could look after her baby. Her husband was able to adjust his work schedule in order to watch the baby in the morning so Lindsay could walk.

So Lindsay hooked the leash on her dog's collar and began walking. After the first day, she told her husband there was no joy in it. She didn't want to walk. Gently her husband encouraged her to take God along on her walks. He suggested she talk to Him as she walked, to cry out, to ask for guidance, to list the blessings He had given and to thank Him for them.

Lindsay said she would try. She began to walk with God. It soon became the most precious time in her day. She returned to the house uplifted and energized for the day ahead. Her walks began to show results: not only did Lindsay get into shape physically, but her time with the Lord got her into good shape spiritually. She became more patient and peaceful. Her joy for life began to reemerge.

There isn't much written in the Bible about Enoch. But we know he walked with God. We are told this twice. And Enoch is mentioned again in the book of Hebrews (11:5–6). Of all the things that could be recorded about this man, God thought it important to tell us of his walk with God not once, but twice.

And Paul mentioned his great faith as an example for believers.

Do you "walk with God"? Is He a part of your daily life? Is He in your thoughts as you go about your day? Do you spend time in His Word, at worship, in prayer?

The peace and patience you so need are found in walking with God each day. You may find the time for a "prayer walk," a time when you actually go for a walk and pray. Or your daily walk may be spent inviting God alongside each thing you do. Either one will result in a closer relationship to the God who sustains and gives life.

Prayer: Lord, I invite You to walk with me today, all day. Thank You for Your presence.

Easy Access

> *Let us therefore come boldly to the throne of grace, that we may obtain mercy and find grace to help in time of need.*
>
> —Hebrews 4:16

It happens to all of us frequently in this modern world: we make a phone call to a place of business and get the "push this number" runaround. There are few things more frustrating in this world than to be in a hurry and have to go through several computerized selections before reaching the desired category. Even then we may not be guaranteed a human voice on the other end of the telephone. Recently, I counted no fewer than seventeen different "push-button" routes before reaching a human being!

I find the same lack of easy access when it comes to trying to reach a specific person in a place of business. Often it is the secretary or personal relations director who intercepts the call. It once took several calls, E-mails, and faxes over a five-day period before I actually heard the voice of the person I sought.

Even the schools my children attend have telephones that are completely automated! I cannot simply call and speak with the secretary to remind them to send my child home on the bus. I must first punch in a series of numbers, punch in a code, and then dial another series of numbers before leaving a message on voice mail. Then I must hope someone retrieves it and puts my child on the bus!

However, there is One whom we never have trouble reaching. God has no "call waiting," no series of numbers to punch, no secretary, no computerized hoops through which to jump. In fact, He is sitting anxiously awaiting our call, ready to spring to our aid when we need Him. We never have to wonder if He gets the message.

We can walk with confidence into His presence at any moment. We can open our eyes in the middle of the night and know He is listening. We can whisper a prayer over the baby napping in the midday shadows and know He is there. We can look up to heaven as we drive our car and immediately enter into conversation with Him.

We have direct access. We have the direct line to His heart. We are His beloved children whom He values above all else. He loves to spend time with us! That's why He created us!

He dances over us in heaven. His heart beats quickly when we so much as think of Him! Right now, He is eagerly awaiting the time He can spend with you. Each day He watches, waiting for your thoughts and words to turn heavenward so that He can have fellowship with you.

No busy signals, no numbers to punch, no one to intercept: just you and the Lord who loves you beyond measure.

Prayer: I am so grateful that You are always there to answer my call. Thank You.

Waiting for Daddy

> *Wait on the LORD;*
> *Be of good courage,*
> *And He shall strengthen your heart;*
> *Wait, I say, on the LORD!*
> —Psalm 27:14

Every evening at 5:00, Kelsey begins her vigil. Her little nose is pressed against the screen of the window, resulting in a delicate crisscross pattern impressed on the tip. Her blue eyes stare at the four lanes of highway down the hill at the end of the driveway. Her blonde curls are lifted by the breezes. Her chubby little fingers grip the windowsill, her toes dance in anticipation. She is distracted by nothing.

She is waiting for her daddy to come home to her. Her anticipation of that joyous moment is so obviously written across her features. Already her eyes sparkle at the thought of his arrival.

I know he is coming when she leaps away from the window

and runs to the door as fast as her little legs can carry her. Squeals of joy spill out of her rosebud lips, and she jumps up and down with her hands on the doorknob. As the knob begins to turn, she backs up, suddenly quiet, her face shining in anticipation.

When her daddy walks in the room, she flings herself into his waiting arms, grabbing his neck and pushing her cheek against his. "Daddy's here! Daddy's here!"

The whole house is warmed by her exuberance. Her daddy is the focus of her day—she asks me repeatedly during the day for the time, anticipating five o'clock. For the first few minutes after her daddy greets her, he kneels before her, listening with rapt attention as she spills forth the details of her day. Then, assured of his love, Kelsey skips off to another adventure.

How I want her joyous anticipation in my own life. Our "Daddy" in heaven will one day arrive for us. What a glorious day it will be when we can fling ourselves into His loving arms and feel His embrace! As He gathers us in, we can let go of the burdens of raising our special children, knowing that all are restored and whole in His presence.

But on a daily basis, we can meet Him, be embraced in His love, and have His rapt attention. He exhorts you to wait upon Him with all the excitement and trust of that little girl waiting for her daddy. He will never fail to come to you.

Let each of us stand on tiptoe, our noses pressed against the screen, awaiting the timing of the Lord in our lives.

Prayer: Lord, I await You: Your timing in my life, Your plans for me and my child, Your embrace, and Your singular attention to my heart's cry.

Taste and See

Taste and see that the LORD is good;
Blessed is the man who trusts in Him!
—Psalm 34:8

Jacob was in intensive care, his little body blue, his heart racing hundreds of beats per minute, threatening to do irreparable damage. Doctors and nurses scrambled for answers, sometimes brushing aside family members who stood fearfully in the doorway of the room.

Jacob's mother moved into a tiny, closet-sized room down the hall. A cot was jammed into the room, angled in order for it to fit. An unused sink hung over the foot of the bed. There was no room for a suitcase, so the mother kept it in her car, walking back and forth to get needed items at night and in the morning.

After two weeks the stress of the situation was getting to everyone. Nurses snapped at the frightened mother, who tried desperately to stay out of their way but overstepped boundaries out of concern for her baby. Everyone needed a break.

She finally promised herself one indulgent half hour each day during which she would treat herself to a cookie in the hospital cafeteria. The cookies were huge and soft, dripping melted chocolate when they were broken. The mother described them as being decadent.

Being prone to compulsive overeating, she knew that the cookie treat could have gotten out of control. The pleasure of the treat had the potential to become a drug used to ease her pain and fear. She could have bought dozens, hoarding them in her little room, eating them in secret. No one would have known, and her body chemistry would have been numbed. But she was aware of her own weaknesses, allowing herself one cookie a day. That moment became her small respite from the isolation room full of monitors, beeps and buzzes, bustling nurses, and fear. She took the time to do some small, pleasurable thing to nurture herself.

There is nothing wrong with our taking some time out for pleasure. God doesn't want us to pine away over our children, busy ourselves with their needs, and lose the pleasures of life. After all, He is the One who gave us the ability to enjoy this world and the wonders within it. He never intended us to be serious every moment of the day.

In His goodness, God gave us laughter and the capacity to enjoy life. He wants us to have fun! I believe He laughs with joy when He sees us laughing. Taste the goodness of the Lord in the joys of this world He has given us, knowing it gives Him pleasure to see us enjoy them.

Just remember that, like anything, we can abuse the gift of pleasure. We can use it as a drug to escape the realities and responsibilities of our lives. Ask the Lord to give you His perspective.

Prayer: Lord, thank You for the little moments of happiness and pleasure You provide during a difficult time.

Giving Up

*Take heed to the ministry which you have received in the Lord,
that you may fulfill it.*

—Colossians 4:17

No one in this world would blame Jackie for wanting to give up. Her life has been filled with incredible trials. Her husband struggled with drug use. When he finally got clean in rehabilitation, their six-year-old daughter was severely injured in a car accident. The little girl lived for another five years with the cognitive abilities of a three- or four-month-old baby. Shortly before her daughter's death, Jackie was diagnosed with cancer and had surgery followed by chemotherapy treatment.

When her daughter died, Jackie entered a profound period of grieving. Within the next few years, Jackie began to doubt her own value, rooted in her own pain. Soon her surviving daughter needed heart surgery. And Jackie faced another mastectomy.

Why go on? she wondered. *I love my daughter and my husband, but . . .* Suicide became an ever-increasing desire.

Jackie didn't realize that she was about to help many women who were struggling through experiences similar to her own.

A friend was riding a bike when she was struck by a car and rendered profoundly disabled. Jackie was uniquely qualified to help the family care for her, having cared for her daughter for so many years. Her friend's children could relax, knowing Jackie was there to help.

Another woman, whose son was born with a severe disability, learned from Jackie to seek the Lord for solace.

Jackie began to share her story, complete with the realization that God had sustained her and strengthened her throughout her ordeals. She was able to tell sorrowing women that God is indeed sovereign—everything that happens in our lives is filtered through His fingers.

"I tell my story so others will know He is a God of mercy and grace. He still showers us with mercy and grace."

Jackie stands as an example of perseverance and God's strength. Through her, God has reached countless women with His call to stand firm, reach out to Him, and trust.

How many hundreds of women would not have been touched by her gentleness and compassion had she given in to her thoughts of suicide? God had a ministry for her that began once she reached the end of herself.

Prayer: Lord, I don't always know what it is You are planning for my life. Help me to stick with Your path so that I can complete the work You've assigned me.

Do Not Forget God

Then beware, lest you forget the LORD who brought you out of the land of Egypt, from the house of bondage.

—Deuteronomy 6:12

Caring for children with differences can be hectic. We, as their mothers, don't follow the same schedules and rules that other mothers may have. We can become so wrapped up in the care of our children that we feel we cannot spare the time to read the Bible or attend a church service.

When we rationalize our reluctance to spend time with God, we are falling into the carefully constructed snare of the devil. Satan doesn't tempt us to hate God. That would be too blatant, too easily dismissed. Rather, the devil's scheme is to make us *forget* God.

If we don't have time for God, we won't get closer to Him. We won't draw our strength from Him. Without the strength of God's Spirit and His Word, we can become powerless, doubting the very source of our strength. We will be much more prone to falling into the temptations set before us by the devil. Eventually, we can fall into bitterness and anger, becoming cold and hard.

We can even risk our very relationship with God. We could become like the ancient Israelites who wandered for years in the desert, unsure and without direction. And, though the Lord will continually pursue us, we will turn to our own ways, follow our own paths, and struggle when there is no need to do so.

We can become apathetic and joyless, frustrated with our lives. Is this the type of woman we want raising our children?

Why tread water when we can be sailing along, skimming the waves as God fills our sails?

We have seen throughout history, and perhaps in our own lives, the hand of God over His people. There is great danger when we forget His faithfulness and mercy.

Prayer: Lord, I refuse to fall into the plot of the devil, who wants me to forget Your goodness. Focus my thoughts on You so that I will never forget Your mercies.

God's Protection   ✦

But the Lord is faithful, who will establish you and guard you from the evil one.

—2 Thessalonians 3:3

Jenny and her husband brought their daughter to a famous clinic in order to get a second opinion. The diagnosis was confirmed. Their daughter, barring the Lord's miraculous intervention, would remain in a vegetative state.

The family had several other children and little in the way of financial resources. Their physicians concurred: their child would be best served in a full-time care facility. After much prayer, Jenny began the heartbreaking task of telling family members their decision.

Soon they were searching for a home for their child. Two were in their area, close enough for the family to visit daily. Jenny and her husband toured the first, the one strongly recommended by their insurance company. They met the staff, saw the rooms, and learned of the various therapies.

When she met the director, Jenny felt a strong urge to flee. She chalked it up to her stress and fatigue. As the man talked about the facility and the special care they provided, Jenny became more and more uncomfortable. Her husband, noticing her distress, asked the director to excuse them for a moment.

Once outside the building, Jenny clutched her husband's hand. "We can't bring her here!" She was as surprised by her words as he was. At the same time, her husband began to feel that this was not the proper place for their child. He entered the building, thanked the director for his time, and left. They placed their daughter in the other facility; one that didn't have quite as much room, or quite as much money, but was filled with loving, cheerful nurses and therapists.

Two weeks later the director of the other facility was arrested for sexually abusing his residents under the age of sixteen.

Jenny firmly believes that God was directing them that day in the hospital. They had prayed for His leading in finding the proper care facility for their daughter, not realizing how strongly the Lord would lead. Their daughter was spared a potentially abusive situation. Jenny and her husband were spared the guilt and grief that would have arisen had their daughter been harmed.

God was guarding them from the evil designs of that man, just as He is guarding and watching over you and your child today. Listen for His voice and heed His leading, for He loves you.

Prayer: Lord, thank You for Your faithfulness and protection in my life.

Butterflies and Rainbows

The rainbow shall be in the cloud, and I will look on it to remember the everlasting covenant between God and every living creature of all flesh that is on the earth.

—Genesis 9:16

God placed a rainbow in the sky as the symbol of His promise to Noah and all the earth that He would never again destroy the earth with a massive flood. Butterflies are cherished by many as a symbol of God's greatest promise to us. Butterflies start out as caterpillars, crawling on the earth. When their time comes, the little worms go into cocoons, waiting silently until they may emerge. When they do, they are transformed into beautiful creatures that float high above the earth.

Butterflies can represent the Christian experience. Right now we are earthbound, moving through life like the caterpillar. We will eventually enter the tomb—just as the little caterpillar enters his cocoon. However, we will emerge transformed by the sacrifice of Jesus. We will drop all chains of this earth and soar with Him in heaven!

Again, the butterfly can represent Christ Himself, who trod upon this earth, toiling as a man. He then died and entered the tomb for our sake, emerging on the other side, having shed His humanity and donned the glorious robes of the perfect Being that He is.

Rainbows and butterflies remind us of God's promises to us.

Penny loved rainbows and butterflies. A gifted little girl, she drew them on every art project she brought home. Her mother saved each one, smiling at the crooked rainbows and floppy-looking butterflies. She knew the drawings were filled with her child's love and wonder.

One afternoon, Penny was severely injured in a car accident, her brain stem damaged beyond repair. The once lively little girl lived only a few more years before God called her home.

Her mother recalls the wonderful moments with her child and clings to the promises of God that she will be reunited with her daughter one day. There will be no trace of the injuries Penny sustained on earth. She will skip among the glories of heaven, perhaps surrounded by rainbows and butterflies. Once again her mother will hear her sweet, clear voice singing, "Jesus loves me, this I know."

It is a promise. And God keeps His promises!

Each time you see a rainbow, or watch a butterfly dance on the breeze, remember the unfailing promises of God. Your child will be whole one day, and through Christ, the two of you can spend eternity singing praises!

Prayer: In every rainbow, Lord, I see Your faithfulness; in every butterfly, Your promise of eternal life with You in heaven.

Make Satan Run!

Resist the devil and he will flee from you.
—James 4:7

Jackie and her husband have a unique perspective on the struggles they have endured. They don't wallow in sorrow over the years spent caring for a daughter whose disabilities, both physical and mental, were profound. They are not bitter. They don't speak in anger about the causes of their daughter's differences. They don't "blame" God. In fact, they don't even have many angry words for the devil who lays obstacles in their path, trying to keep them from God.

When asked why they aren't angry, they explain that God is sovereign. He is a good and loving God who has their best interests at heart.

They speak of the fallen world and its frailties. And they speak of the devil whose hand may have been at work in the trials they have encountered. Jackie laughs as she relates her husband's attitude. She says that he simply sticks out his tongue at the devil and says, "You want me to buckle under, but everything you throw at me brings me closer to God." And Satan runs away like a whipped dog with his tail between his legs!

We are not helpless in the face of temptation and adversity! We have power over the devil when we call on the name of God. When we resist the temptation of the devil, he doesn't walk away. Scripture says he *flees*—frightened and beaten. That power is renewed with every trial, every obstacle.

Today, when things are hard with your special child, when you think you can't continue, when bitterness threatens, when temptation pulls at you, remember the opportunity you have before you! You can defeat the devil and walk even closer to God!

Refusal to do so is also our choice. The challenge is whether to accept the victory over the devil that God provides, or to succumb to the mockery of power that the devil seizes. All you need do is make the choice: God will provide the means to overcome.

Prayer: Lord, today I stand in Your victory over the devil. You have triumphed! When I call on Your name, the devil must flee! Help me to live in Your victory!

Small Mercies

(For the LORD your God is a merciful God) He will not forsake you nor destroy you.

—Deuteronomy 4:31

Angela looks back with gratitude on the years of struggle during which she cared for her severely disabled daughter. Her child had been perfectly healthy for almost seven years, but after a serious car accident, she became totally dependent on others during her last five years on earth.

The Lord gifted Angela with several precious moments of remembrance before taking her little one home to heaven.

The week before the child's mind was taken, her teacher called Angela to relate a warm story showing her daughter's obvious love for others: a little boy in her daughter's class was disabled, requiring him to use a walker for support when he walked. During recess the little boy would watch the other children play kick-ball. He never spoke, but simply watched longingly as the other children laughed and interacted. No one played with him. No one even seemed to notice him there.

When Angela's daughter was allowed to select the game for recess, she grabbed the ball and approached the little boy, who had already positioned himself in his usual lonely spot. He looked up to see her bright smile as she asked him to play. She positioned herself on the ground and asked him to play "hot potato" with her. It was a game he could play!

Soon all of the children in her class had joined the two of them, their collective laughter ringing out across the afternoon sky. The phone call was the last before Angela lost the sparkling little girl to a severe mental disability. The memory warms her heart. It was a small mercy.

Angela believes it was that same gift of compassion that her daughter displayed the day she left this life. She became seriously ill on May 18, which was her sister's tenth birthday. Though seriously ill, she clung to life until the early hours of May 19. Angela believes that her daughter refused to die on her sister's birthday, which would have forever tainted the day with an edge of sadness. This also was a small mercy.

So many times the Lord allows these simple mercies to occur, giving us just enough to cling to in order to weather the sorrow around us. Scripture says that God's mercies are new every morning. He stands ever ready with forgiveness, compassion, and love. He gifts each day with its share of His mercies—little encounters and uplifting times.

Look around you as you move through your day today. Watch for the little mercies the Lord places in your path to brighten your day. When you are looking for them, you will be amazed at how many you will discover.

Prayer: Lord, thank You for Your small mercies. Help me to see them today.

Small World . . . Or a Big God? ✷

The LORD sat enthroned at the Flood,
And the LORD sits as King forever.
　　　　　　　　　　—Psalm 29:10 NKJV

God knows what He is doing. He orchestrates our lives and moves people into our paths long before we even know we need them. The year before having our first child, we moved to a new city. I was lonely, missing the church I had left, unable to find one like it. With relief, I discovered a Christian radio station that played the type of music I liked. The station also included solid, biblical teachings from men and women of God around the country. Three times a day, the station had "prayer time," a time when they prayed over the prayer requests that had been phoned or mailed in to the station.

It was during prayer time that I learned of a girl named Penny who had been in a catastrophic accident and clung to life with little hope of full recovery. The plight of this little girl and the unnamed family stayed with me for years. I prayed diligently for them.

Three years later, I found the church home for which I had been searching. At several services I saw a family with a little girl in a wheelchair. She was on a ventilator and seemed to have little recognition of where she was. But she loved the music at worship. Each day that I saw her, I breathed a prayer for her and her family.

As I became more involved in the church, I met Jeanne, a wonderful Christian servant. Jeanne introduced me to her sister, Jackie. Jackie and I had an easy rapport. She was kind and gentle. I began giving piano lessons to her daughter. After a while I learned that Jackie had another daughter, Penny.

Of course, Penny had been the little girl for whom I had been praying for years. Jackie told me of the miracles of Penny's life, the people who had come to know God through her, the fact that she should have been in excruciating pain for her final days–but wasn't. "It was prayer that sustained us."

When my youngest was born with differences, Jackie was one of the first to tell me she was praying for him.

God's plan had come full circle.

Prayer: Lord, You orchestrate our lives in accordance to Your perfect plan. We need not be surprised at the completeness thereof.

Miracles   ✹

> *For I am the LORD, I do not change.*
> —Malachi 3:6

Our God is still a God of miracles. He still has the power to perform them when they are in accordance to His will. Some of the miracles in our lives are quiet little moments of His grace. Other miracles may be huge, bringing us to our knees in awe.

One mother I know received a miracle that seemed straight out of the Old Testament. When she told me of it, she asked if I remembered the story of the poor widow and her son who took in Elijah and fed him with the last of her flour and oil. Her flour and oil were plentiful until the Lord stopped the drought. I remembered the story. My friend then told me of a small bottle of oil she had been given to anoint her daughter. She used it during evening prayers as she prayed over the little girl's broken body, anointing the child's forehead, hands, and chest. Her nurses used the oil to anoint her when they bathed her.

During the long months in the hospital, the oil was never used up.

Another mother knew many people were praying for her child who had been born with a severe craniofacial deformity. The baby's pediatrician had examined the child and shook his head, expressing concern over the wide rifts in the bone structure of the baby's face. It would be many years, and many surgeries, before that hole could be closed.

Two months later, the baby was again brought to the pediatrician's office for a preoperative examination. The doctor became very quiet as he examined the boy. Finally he turned to the mother with a confused look. "Bone has grown here . . . the hole is almost shut." As they discussed the phenomenon, the doctor admitted that he had never seen anything as profound in his career.

Mike was a bitter and angry man. He was enmeshed in a drug lifestyle, ignoring his family and his job. When his daughter became disabled, God turned his life around. Mike began searching for God, finding a deep, personal relationship with Him. The Mike of today is very little like the man he was before he had a disabled child. His wife speaks freely of the miracle God performed in changing the hard, bitter man into one of tenderness and compassion.

Sometimes God chooses to perform His miracles in full view of others. Sometimes He works them in the deep recesses of our hearts. But He still performs them, just as faithfully as He always has.

Prayer: You are a God of miracles, the same today as You always have been, as You always will be. Perform Your miracles today in my heart and my life as I give them to You for safe-keeping. Please do the same for my precious child.

Caring for His Own

When my father and my mother forsake me,
Then the LORD will take care of me.
—Psalm 27:10

Lynn will never live independently. She is nearly forty years old and mentally disabled. She is a wonderful woman with a childlike mind. Lynn loves Jesus. She loves coming to church with her family, and she loves playing with her nieces and nephews.

When Lynn's mother became ill, concern was raised over what would become of Lynn. Her brother and sister each had several children, and neither had an income sufficient to cover Lynn's special needs. Secretly, Lynn's sister hoped that she would not have to deal with the added stress of caring for her sister.

Lynn's mother died, having left a small sum of money to help with Lynn's care. With that sum and other benefits provided by the government, Lynn would be well provided for—once a permanent home was found for her. The brother and sister took her into their homes temporarily while searching for another place for Lynn to live.

Finally they decided she should live in a resident facility outside of the city. Living there would mean Lynn would not be able to attend her church. She would not be able to help in the toddler Sunday school classes. She wouldn't be at the church functions and concerts. Lynn was very sad that first Sunday in her new home. She didn't seem much happier as the weeks turned into months.

Meanwhile, at the church, people began to notice Lynn's absence. Finally, one woman asked the pastor if he knew where Lynn had been during the past few months. He told them of her new home outside of the city. He also mentioned how sad Lynn seemed when he visited her.

This woman began to call others in the church, forming a group of dedicated women who committed themselves to driving out to Lynn's new home and bringing her to church each Sunday. Almost immediately, the residential care workers noticed a vast improvement in Lynn's demeanor. She began to become involved in activities at the residence. She sang and laughed and played. When she was asked about the difference in her mood, Lynn told everyone that she was able to visit Jesus again, and that made her happy. When Lynn's life was changed by the loss of her mother, the Lord set people in place to care for her. He knew she needed that time each Sunday to spend with Him and the others in the church.

Don't despair over the future. The Lord will take care of you and your child. Even when those closest to you step away, He is still there. All the resources of the universe are at His fingertips to distribute for the care of His own. All we need do is ask.

Prayer: Lord, I know that no matter where we are in life, no matter how alone we may feel, You are there to take care of us. Thank You for Your constant care.

Not Ashamed

He is not ashamed to call them brethren, saying:
"I will declare Your name to My brethren;
In the midst of the assembly I will sing praise to You.

—Hebrews 2:11–12

A pastor tells of growing up with two mentally disabled siblings. As a child, he would be mercilessly teased by the other children at school. The teasing hurt him to the point that he became angry at God and ashamed of his brother and sister. In his anger and shame, he turned to drugs and fast living.

Quietly and gently, God began to call him, coaxing the man toward a relationship with Him. Finally, confused and aimless, the man turned his life over to God, eventually becoming a pastor and teacher, leading many to find the same rewarding relationship with Jesus that he had found.

The pastor is not proud of his past shame over his siblings. He loves them dearly and always has. But there were times when he felt deep shame over their differences. There were times when he was ashamed to have them as siblings.

Isn't it ironic that Jesus does not express shame over us? So many of us are far more damaged than our children, and yet He is not ashamed to call us brethren. We are sinful and can be selfish and proud; we hurt Him and turn away from Him. We may abuse drugs and alcohol, we may overeat or over-indulge in myriad vices. We may live with hidden sin in our lives. Yet He calls us His brothers and sisters, unashamed.

There may be times when we feel shame over our child's

differences. That is human. We struggle against our human nature every day. Confess it to the Lord, and ask His aid in quieting those feelings. Your child has no difference over which you should feel shame. God formed your little one into His image. When you are tempted to feel shame, call to mind the fact that every person you know, every person you meet, *everyone* is damaged and lacks perfection.

But the Lord feels no shame in calling them brethren. That includes you. And that includes your child.

Prayer: Lord, You are not ashamed to call me Your sister. Help me never to be ashamed to claim my child, no matter the circumstance. Likewise, and most important, help me to never feel ashamed to claim You.

Questioning His Maker

Woe to him who strives with his Maker!
Let the potsherd strive with the potsherds of the earth!
Shall the clay say to him who forms it, "What are you making?"
Or shall your handiwork say, "He has no hands"?

—Isaiah 45:9

Jim's mother had taken thalidomide during her pregnancy with him. The drug helped with morning sickness. What no one realized at the time was that the drug also caused severe birth defects. Jim was born with small hands that grew from his shoulders. His legs were severely misshapen and bent.

All of his life, Jim was bitter over the blow that "fate" had dealt him. He refused to learn a useful trade, claiming that he was unable to do anything of use to the world. He refused offers of friendship. He lashed out angrily at family members. He shook his head and cursed God, asking Him why He had made him a "monster." Most of all he cursed his mother for her part in his differences.

His mother, having suffered with guilt and anger, finally turned to God, finding peace and compassion at last. Eventually, she was able to release the guilt she felt over her son. And she learned to forgive him for his outbursts of anger and the bitterness he harbored toward her.

Jim had no desire to forgive his mother, no matter how innocent she had been. He seemed to have no desires at all. His mother grew increasingly frustrated over the hardness of her son's heart. She began to pray earnestly, asking the Lord to soften her son and shake loose his anger.

One day as Jim was watching television with his mother, a live broadcast showed the arrival of the pope at a youth conference in the United States. Onstage a young man played guitar. The music was indescribably beautiful. The pope was so moved, he approached the young man and kissed him. Jim turned to his mother, his eyes filled with tears, his mouth quivering. "I'm so sorry," he choked out as his mother wrapped her arms around him. They wept, clinging to each other. From that day, the two of them discovered a new and wonderful relationship. Jim eventually received forgiveness from the Lord and began a new life in Him.

Years later, Jim's mother still cries tears of joy when describing that telecast. She and Jim had been listening to the music but not watching closely. When the pope had approached the young man, Jim made the comment, "That guitarist is really good!" It was only when the camera moved to a close-up that Jim and his mother saw that the guitarist had no arms. He had played that beautiful music with his feet.

Jim at last had come to know that his anger and bitterness had been a form of questioning God's sovereignty. He learned instead to trust Him. God knows better than any of us what He is doing.

Prayer: Lord, I will not question You today. I will instead trust that Your plan and Your designs are perfect. You are my Maker. You have formed my child. We are Yours.

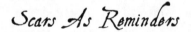

Scars As Reminders

See, I have inscribed you on the palms of My hands.

—Isaiah 49:16

Quiana is ten years old now. She has begun asking her mother about the scars that cross her body, both on her chest and on her back. The scars are deep and long. They are not beautiful. They have been there since the day of her birth.

Quiana had been born with a rare and not fully understood condition where the bottom of her esophagus was attached to her trachea, a "mix-up" in the tubing. As a result food would go to Quiana's lungs. This condition (known as TEF/EA) occurs in only 1 in 5,000 births. In an attempt to save her life, Quiana had her first surgery within twelve hours of birth. She has had four more surgeries since then. There is the possibility that she will have more during her lifetime.

The scars were incurred during the surgeries that saved her life. Some are the result of the feeding tubes and drainage tubes she had to wear for a time. Quiana's mother tells her daughter that the scars do not make her different from other children, but that they are reminders that God was able to help the doctors to heal her. The scars are proof that she is loved.

Jesus bears scars too. His scars are the result of His death on the cross for us. The scars mark His feet and His side and His hands. They were put there by the nails that held Him to the cross. They were placed by the spear that pierced His side. They are constant reminders of His great love for us.

There is a significant difference between the scars on Quiana and those on the hands and feet of our Lord: Quiana's scars are the result of doctors saving *her* life; Jesus' scars are the result of Him saving *ours*.

Picture the palms of His hands. Those wounds into which Thomas was invited to place his hands are still there. Look closely and see that the scars are not in the shape of the nails. They are in the form of letters. They are the letters of your name. They are the letters of your child's name. The Lord has inscribed your names permanently on His hands. He has carved them deeply into His heart, and He will never, ever forget you.

Prayer: Lord, You have inscribed me into the palm of Your hand. You hold my child and me in those capable and scarred hands. Help me to rest in that security today. Help me to see the scars on my child and on my heart as reminders of Your deep concern and love.

Poured Out As an Offering

Yes, and if I am being poured out as a drink offering on the sacrifice and service of your faith, I am glad and rejoice with you all.
—Philippians 2:17

We can look back upon the lives of many who suffered for the gain of others. Mother Teresa is a great example of a woman who lived a painful life, especially toward the end, but toiled on without complaint in order to help others both physically and spiritually. We can only begin to guess at the number of souls who will spend eternity in heaven with the Lord because her life sparked them out of complacency and sinfulness and made them curious about God.

Mother Teresa's life was poured out in the service of the most destitute of people on earth. And information about this humble servant was made known around the world, reaching many of the most destitute souls on earth.

I think Mother Teresa would have been surprised to see how many lives were affected by her humble example. Many have been spurred to greater acts of service, some entering the mission field, some serving quietly in their own homes and neighborhoods.

We, too, have a unique opportunity to model Christ in our lives. Because of our children's differences, we can come under close scrutiny at times. People with no experience in our situation may take a moment to imagine raising a child with a disability.

Jen has four children, all under the age of six. Her oldest has

Down's syndrome. As Jen shopped one afternoon for groceries, her children were noisily "helping." Jen explained to her oldest daughter again and again that she could not put just anything she wanted in the cart. She would hand the item to her daughter and help her replace it on the shelf.

A woman approached Jen. "You're a saint!" the woman exclaimed. Jen turned a patient smile toward the woman. "Thank you for your kind words, but any patience or endurance I have comes from the Lord, who has given me four wonderful children . . . and the strength to chase after them!" she responded. The woman thought a moment and then smiled. "What a wonderful way to live your life."

How right that woman is. When we realize the Source of our strength, we are then in a position to be living examples of His grace and strength. We can give our lives as offerings to strengthen the faith of those who see us. And if that sacrifice is recognized aloud, we can direct their admiration toward the One who truly deserves it, for it is only through the Lord that we can endure and overcome this world.

Prayer: Lord, my life is an offering poured out in service to You and others. Use my unique situation to point others toward You.

Blessings in Common Ground

For it has been declared to me concerning you, my brethren . . .
that there are contentions among you . . . Is Christ divided?
—1 Corinthians 1:11, 13

Paul expressed concern over the divisions in the Corinthian church. He did not want to see the church arguing. The Lord grieves over this today as well.

The day before Eileen's son was to have his first surgery, a neighbor knocked on the door. She held in her hand a small plastic vial. Giving it to Eileen, the neighbor explained that it was holy water from a site in France, believed to be sacred by those in her church. Eileen, who did not share the same beliefs of her neighbor, did, however, recognize the loving motivations behind the gift.

Her neighbor believed the water had the power to bless and heal the baby. She was giving it in the spirit of hope, risking ridicule or possibly anger if the gift was seen as offensive.

Eileen began to cry, touched by the compassion and concern of her neighbor for her little boy. Eileen related the story of how her mother had received water from the same site in France thirty years earlier when her fifth child was in danger. Eileen explained that although she was deeply touched by the gift, she did not share the woman's belief in the power of the water. With deep respect for each other's beliefs, the two women shared together their love for Christ and His people. They spent time that day explaining the doctrines of their churches, reading Scripture, and praying together. Each recognized the core relationship in their lives—that of receiving Christ as Savior and Lord—as being the most important shared experience between them.

The two women, though still separate on doctrinal elements of their faith, have grown close in the fellowship of Christians. That neighbor is one of the first people Eileen calls for prayer when her son has another surgery.

When others see the differences in our children, they may reach out to us in ways that conflict with our personal beliefs or even with the very Scriptures. In those moments, we have the opportunity to speak truth while acknowledging the loving motivation of their hearts. We can build a relationship, while gently steering them toward Scripture and truth, or we can destroy any chance of relationship by rejecting the gift and the person giving it.

Look to the example of Jesus, who gently led while never compromising truth.

Prayer: Lord, help me to see the common ground that believers share in You even when our doctrines do not agree.

Is There No Balm?

> *Is there no balm in Gilead,*
> *Is there no physician there?*
> *Why then is there no recovery*
> *For the health of the daughter of my people?*
> —Jeremiah 8:22

God is the Great Physician. He will heal when it is in accordance to His plan. Sometimes He will do so with stunning power, leaving skeptics grasping for answers that are not forthcoming. Many times He will use the giftedness of doctors and nurses to bring about a slower healing. Sometimes the physical healing will occur in heaven. Sometimes He heals the body. Sometimes He heals the heart.

I am sure that every one of us who is raising a child with differences has cried out at some time for a miracle. We want our children to be healed. It is a natural desire borne of our deep love for our little ones. Many times in the dark of night, I have wept and pleaded with God for His divine intervention to heal my son so that he can be like so many other children who do not have to endure surgery after surgery, so that his face will look like other faces and he will be saved from the stares and teasing of others.

In each of those times, I have felt the presence of God assuring me that His plan is not to harm my child, but to give him hope and a future. I am learning, bit by bit, to trust His timing and not my own.

In the process, God has healed many of the hurts that I carried within. The present struggles brought out issues from my past that had never been healed—things that prevented me from fully trusting the Lord. Little by little, God has healed those wounds, bringing me to a place of trust and security in Him.

At the same time, God is healing my son. Few people notice his scars, thanks to the giftedness of his plastic surgeon. With each surgery and speech therapy, Aiden's speech becomes more and more clear. In only two years, my child has been transformed from the baby whose face caused people to recoil, to the little charmer who draws a crowd of admirers.

God is faithfully healing both of us . . . in His perfect time.

Prayer: Lord, Your timing is perfect. Give me the patience to trust in that timing. You are the balm in Gilead who soothes, comforts, and heals—both inside and out. You are the Great

Physician who guides the physicians who work on my child. I place our care in Your hands.

Growing Through the Rocks

Consider the lilies of the field, how they grow: they neither toil nor spin; and yet I say to you that even Solomon in all his glory was not arrayed like one of these. Now if God so clothes the grass of the field, which today is, and tomorrow is thrown into the oven, will He not much more clothe you?

—Matthew 6:28–30

I have one stubborn daffodil in my yard. I don't know how it got where it is; I certainly did not plant it there! And yet, spring after spring, it lifts its golden head and sways merrily in the wind.

My other daffodils are lined up neatly in a flower bed, nicely banked, thoroughly weeded. The rogue flower is in the middle of an area covered with landscaping rocks. Each spring the flower must push the red stones aside to make room for its growth. I do nothing to help the flower: I do not pull weeds away, I do not water it nor do I feed it. But it continues to grow, huge and bright against the dark stones. It doesn't know that the odds are against its survival. No one takes care of that flower but the Lord.

I have found myself looking for that flower each spring, waiting with almost bated breath to see if it has persevered one more year. And, unfailingly, it is there.

Jesus pointed out the beauty of the flowers, reminding us that God made them more beautiful than the clothing of the richest man who ever lived. In the same chapter He told us about how the Lord takes care of the wild birds, feeding them and keeping them alive although they do not plant or reap or store food in barns.

We can learn a lot from the little rogue flower. It shows us that the beauty of God's creation can spring up in the most unlikely of places. It proves that God is faithful in His care of the flowers, clothing and feeding them. It shows us the rewards of perseverance.

Look into your own life with your child. Can you see the beauty that reveals itself in the most unlikely places? Do you see the faithfulness of God in His care and provision? Are you seeing the rewards of perseverance?

Many times, when we stop to think about it, all of these become apparent in and through the lives of our children. Some of the rewards may come to light after we enter into His presence for eternity. But many are here today.

Take a moment to consider the rogue flower in your life— your child—the one who is growing before your eyes, despite whatever may threaten. And remember the One who cares for the rogue flower, bringing His plans to perfect completion.

Prayer: Lord, thank You for Your promises in chapter 6 of Matthew. Today I place my worries into Your hands, knowing that You are my Provider.

A Parent's Love

The LORD your God in your midst,
The Mighty One, will save;
He will rejoice over you with gladness,
He will quiet you with His love,
He will rejoice over you with singing.
—Zephaniah 3:17

My children and I went to the local high school for a football game one Friday night. The stands were packed with cheering fans. There were as many adults there as there were teenagers from the school.

At halftime, the parents were introduced. They walked onto the field as their names were announced, holding a sign with their son's name and jersey number. The cheerleaders escorted their own parents onto the field. The parents stood with pride, showing the crowd their connection to their son or daughter.

During the remainder of the game, I became more and more aware of parents calling out their son's names. I heard cries of "That's my boy!"

It is normal to be proud of our children. I sit in darkened auditoriums with tear-filled eyes as I watch my beautiful daughter dance. Those same tears are present when my twins try their best on the ball field. They are there when my littlest girl sings a song from Sunday school. And they flowed this week as my youngest said his first "g" sound after years of speech therapy.

I am one of those mothers who carries pictures of her children, ever ready to show others the wonderful little ones God has placed in my care.

Did you know that the Lord exults over you and your child in the same manner? He sees our small steps toward Him and cheers for us! He beams as He looks upon us, His children. He is proud of you. He is proud of your child. You are both exactly the persons He created you to be. He loves you with an immeasurable love.

The Lord stands proudly over you, calling out, "That's My girl!" He proudly proclaims His connection to you as your Father. I wouldn't be surprised if His wallet is packed with pictures . . .

Prayer: Lord, although at times it is difficult to grasp, I know You love my child more than I ever could. Help me to also accept the fact that You love me in the same complete manner. During this day, fill me with the knowledge of that overwhelming love.

Anger

"Be angry, and do not sin": do not let the sun go down on your wrath, nor give place to the devil.

—Ephesians 4:26–27

Feel your anger. Vent it in a safe place. Tell the Lord you are angry. Let out a primal scream in a private place. Acknowledge your anger over the injustices of this life.

The Bible does not say, "Don't be angry." It gives us permission to feel this human emotion. However, it has a qualifier: do not sin. It is OK to be angry. It is not OK to use anger as an excuse to sin against God and other people.

Do you have a right to be angry over the special needs of your child? Of course you do! No doubt God is angry that children must suffer in myriad ways. That was never His plan for His creation. But with the fall of Adam, we entered a world where sin ruled and only by the grace of God could we avoid falling into it. And the only way to receive that grace and strength is to receive the sacrifice and lordship of Jesus Christ in our lives.

And even once that is done, we will still suffer in this world. Some of that suffering may be the consequences of our own sinful actions. Some of it may be God's way of drawing us to a closer relationship with Him. Some of it may be the attack of the devil and his minions, whose only desire is to hurt God by destroying us.

Do not give the devil a foothold by turning to sin when you suffer. Picture a safe and solid wooden door standing between you and the devil. That door is Jesus. The devil cannot open the door no matter how hard he tries. He cannot get to you when you hide behind the Lord. However, if in your suffering you crack open that door to sin, he slides his foot in the crack, holding it open. Unless we turn again to the Lord in repentance, that door stays ajar. Little by little the devil can slide in a bit farther. Then a little more. Eventually, he would be able to pass through and do serious damage to our relationship with God. It becomes much more difficult for us to shut the door the farther we allow it to open.

When you feel angry over the situation you find yourself or your precious child in, turn to the Lord. Talk to Him rather than crack that door.

Prayer: Lord, stay solidly between me and the tricks of the devil. Help me to turn to You with my anger. Keep me from falling into the temptation to sin when I am in the midst of that tempest.

No Separation

> *For I am persuaded that neither death nor life, nor angels nor principalities nor powers, nor things present nor things to come, nor height nor depth, nor any other created thing, shall be able to separate us from the love of God which is in Christ Jesus our Lord.*
> —Romans 8:38–39

"God loves you." She remembers the note clearly. She had been riding a bus for more than an hour and was still another hour from her destination. She had huddled close to the window, staring vacantly at the brittle landscape. Eventually so much frost had formed on the outside of the window that she could no longer see through it. It didn't matter; her mind was turned inward, trying to make sense of the life in which she now found herself.

Every now and then a tear would drip from her chin onto her heavy winter coat. She was sure no one was watching, that no one cared. She wasn't even feeling too sure that God cared, either. Oh, she believed God cared about everyone else. She was just trying to figure out if He still cared for her.

She had spent the previous months turning away from God's love. His gentle urgings were ignored. She was angry with Him over the most recent assessments of her son. She was tired. She was stressed and depressed. Above all, she was angry.

She had spent the first hour of the trip contemplating escape: running away, dipping into the haze of drugs and alcohol, or suicide. She had been a believer for more than fifteen years, and yet when her world was shaken, she began to look to the world for solutions. Then the note, carefully folded, landed in her lap. She looked up only to see the back of the man who dropped it as he made his way to the back of the bus. She opened the paper. "God loves you." It hit her like a lightning bolt. It rang true, and at last she believed it.

She realized that God had pursued her, trying again and again to convince her of His great love. He finally had to put it into writing to get her attention! She had tried so hard to separate herself from that love.

The Bible says that no created thing can separate you from the love of God. That includes you. You are a created being, and no matter what you may do to separate yourself from Him, God will still love you with an enduring, encompassing love.

Are you running from that love? Stop. Let Him gather you close and love you today.

Prayer: Lord, it is amazing to realize that nothing I can do will ever stop Your love for me and my child. Thank You for the security in knowing that You will always love me, no matter what may happen.

Puzzle Pieces

God had planned something better for us so that only together with us would they be made perfect.

—Hebrews 11:40 NIV

Susan loves jigsaw puzzles. It is her favorite hobby, one she pursues with a passion she rarely displays elsewhere. Each new puzzle is a fresh challenge for her, to be attacked with great enthusiasm and anticipation.

Susan worked for months in her spare time putting together a very large and complex jigsaw puzzle. What had begun as a chaotic pile of mismatched colors was coming together more and more each day into a beautiful picture. Susan watched with excitement as the finished picture became more clear.

She called one day in tears. When I asked what was wrong, Susan told me that the puzzle was missing a piece right in the middle of the picture. She had looked around the room and under the furniture. She had scoured the entire house, hoping the piece would turn up in another room. She had even emptied the bag on her vacuum cleaner. The piece was lost. The picture was forever marred and incomplete.

Life is like one of those puzzles. We begin it with high hopes and excitement and then settle in to the long days of fitting together the pieces. As we age, the picture becomes more and more clear as God completes our lives.

Each one of us is a puzzle piece in the larger picture of God's plan. We interact and fit together with those around us to build the picture God is painstakingly putting together. He moves each piece to just the right position and then fits it into place. Your little one is a piece of this puzzle, purposed from the beginning to fit exactly the puzzle God is currently building. Without your special child, the puzzle would be incomplete, forever marred by that absence.

There was no mistake when your child was created. There is a spot meant just for that child in God's great puzzle—a spot only your child can fill. And when all of the pieces are in place the picture will be more beautiful than any puzzle we ever could have imagined.

Prayer: Lord, thank You for the unique place You have purposed for my child in this life. Only my child can fit the plan You have made for us. Thank You for fitting together the pieces of our lives.

Transforming

And do not be conformed to this world, but be transformed by the renewing of your mind, that you may prove what is that good and acceptable and perfect will of God.

—Romans 12:2

Pastor John was called to the hospital one evening. A lovely little girl lay in the white bed, pale and still, her hair fanning across the crisp pillow. Her eyes were closed, her breathing shallow. Marci was in a diabetic coma.

The pastor pulled up a chair and began praying for the little girl. He knew the doctors had given the family little hope that Marci would recover. Pastor John felt a kinship to this little girl in that he, too, has diabetes.

For hours this gentle man held Marci and stroked her hair, praying fervently for her health to return. After a long night, Pastor John began to sense a change. He gazed at Marci and was literally able to watch the life flow back into this little girl. Within days she had made a complete recovery. Pastor John marvels still at the transformation he witnessed that dark night: a little girl on the brink of death was transformed into a bubbling, bright-eyed child right before his eyes.

We can witness the same transformation in our own lives when we allow the Lord to renew our spirit. As we stand before Him, nearly dead inside with the spirit-crushing burdens of our children's differences, we can pray as fervently as Pastor John for God's life-giving spirit to flow through us. We can be pulled from the brink of spiritual death to the bubbling fullness of life that only the Lord can supply.

Those around us can watch in wonder, just as Pastor John did, as the evidence of spiritual renewal flows through us. Our children will see us become more patient, more even tempered, more peaceful. The turmoil inside will become less chaotic and we will have a new sense of leading. In turn, our relationships will change, becoming more like what God desires them to be. Our households will continue this change as separating walls tumble down.

Pray for renewal today—renewal within the confines of your own heart. Let that be the starting point for a new and wonderful relationship with the Lord, who loves you beyond compare.

Prayer: Lord, renew my heart, fill me with Your Spirit. Cleanse me and change me to become more like You. Lead me and teach me in the way that You would have me go. I yield my heart today to You.

A Greater Good

All the paths of the LORD are mercy and truth,
To such as keep His covenant and His testimonies.

—Psalm 25:10

Life may take a curious path when we cannot see the bigger picture. God's perspective is eternal. Ours is finite, moored in the present, with little hope of complete understanding of God's plans.

Jackie was a licensed practical nurse, working at a career she loved. She had two beautiful little girls. And, though her husband was battling his own war with substance abuse, he was still providing for them. Jackie attended church and had a circle of friends. Except for the "usual" challenges, life seemed good to Jackie.

It took one instant and an inattentive driver to shatter Jackie's finite perspective. In that moment she lost her older daughter to almost complete disability, which led to her death a few years later. Her younger daughter, traumatized both physically and emotionally, would never be the same. To add a final despairing touch to the situation, Jackie was injured to the point that she could no longer practice the profession she so loved.

Jackie wondered how this could ever be "true and merciful." She saw it as being just one final insult heaped on the tragedy that had befallen her family.

Jackie did not see until many years later that her injury in the accident was a blessing in disguise. Had she been able-bodied, Jackie would not have been able to use her training to help her daughter. Instead she would have been working, paying bills, and delegating the everyday nursing to hired help. Jackie was perfectly trained to be an advocate for her daughter, fighting for changes in hospital and insurance policies that have the potential to help thousands of families.

Her accident opened the door for a greater dependence on God and others. She learned to become one of an entire body of believers who helped each other whenever necessary. After her daughter's death, Jackie felt called to a new ministry—one in which her experience and compassion were called upon. She began helping others learn to cope with traumatic accidents, caring for others in their homes. Because she cannot work full-time as an LPN, she has the time to reach out and minister to others.

Her husband, who has received treatment for his addictions, has joined her in serving the church. Their relationship with God and each other has blossomed into full flower.

Prayer: Lord, we don't always understand Your paths, but You know where You are going! Help us to continue trusting You as You lead us with mercy and truth.

He So Loves You

For God so loved the world that He gave His only begotten Son, that whoever believes in Him should not perish but have everlasting life.

—John 3:16

The little girl looked up innocently into her mother's eyes. "Momma, you know Jesus loves you, don't you?"

It was an innocent question, yet the mother hesitated. Did she know this? Really? She murmured a reply meant to pacify the girl, who skipped away, not knowing it would be her last day on earth to play. *Does Jesus really love me?* the mother thought. She was about to find out.

In retrospect, the mother sees the question as being perfectly timed. It caused her discomfort, but she could not forget it that night as she watched her little girl battle for her life in the hospital. It echoed through her mind as she cleaned tracheostomy tubes and feeding tubes. It thundered around her as she moved through years of caring for her daughter.

At times she wanted to scream out, "No! He couldn't possibly love me and abandon me like this!" But, gradually, she began to see His loving hand around her. She saw the people praying for her. She received their calls, gifts of service, and their letters. She noticed the "coincidences" that allowed her to be with her daughter. She felt the peace she could never fully explain.

Finally, confronted in love by her sister, the mother of this little girl prayed for Jesus to be Lord of her life. Her life became flooded with His love and mercy. She came to realize that Jesus did indeed love her. He wept with her and rejoiced with her, standing with her through every struggle and joy. Yes, she can now proclaim, I *know* that Jesus loves me.

Do you know Jesus loves you? There are days that you may not believe this truth. Some days may be difficult and painful. During these times remember that Jesus went through agony, both physically and spiritually, to pay ransom for you. He loves you more than you can ever understand, and He longs for your love in return.

Allow your difficulties to be the catalyst that brings you to Him. He awaits with open arms to draw you near so that He may fill you with His love.

Prayer: Lord, it may be difficult for us to receive Your love, a love that is pure and trustworthy and unfailing. Teach us how to open our hearts to You. Right now, I take the time to sit quietly and receive from You the love You so readily give.

He Can Forgive Anything

As far as the east is from the west,
So far has He removed our transgressions from us.

—Psalm 103:12

As mothers we are easy prey for the lies of the devil when it comes to our special children. The king of liars will whisper into our ears, blaming us for the differences in our children. He will hiss that we are terrible mothers when we are tired and wish for a moment that our children were no longer a burden. He will smirk with satisfaction as we sink into guilt over our thoughts and actions. And he knows our guilt can run deepest when it concerns our children. Self-contempt is one of his best weapons against the children of God.

We are "supposed" to be devoted and kind and patient and loving, going about our day without complaint. But our human nature may allow our fatigue to bring forth ugly thoughts. You are not alone if you have wished that you could just run away and never return. And many mothers have had moments in which they wished their child was no longer alive. Each has sunk into the despair of guilt, wondering what kind of mother they have become.

But we have a merciful and understanding Father who can forgive anything we bring to Him in a spirit of repentance.

Julie went beyond wishing her child was gone. Julie actually did something about it. Weak from the cancer that had ravaged her own body, Julie felt as though she just could not continue caring for her profoundly disabled daughter. She was so very tired and depressed. One night, Julie administered an overdose of medication to her daughter. Her knowledge as a medical professional told her that the medication was more than enough to end her daughter's life. Julie didn't even have the energy to care if she was caught and punished.

But God, in His mercy, nudged Julie from the devil's snare. She hurried her daughter to the hospital and told them what she had done. The doctors hurried into action, treating her daughter. Later that evening, blood tests failed to show any medication in her daughter's system. Julie was spared legal ramifications, and her actions that night frightened her into seeking help for her depression.

She fell to her knees before God and asked His forgiveness. She, in turn, requested the same from her daughter and her husband. In time, she came to a place of forgiveness and healing, with a firm knowledge of the wickedness of the devil's lies.

Prayer: (Spend a moment telling God about your private guilt or sin. Ask for His forgiveness, and then take a moment to sit quietly and receive it.)

Empty Arms

> *Therefore my spirit is overwhelmed within me;*
> *My heart within me is distressed.*
> —Psalm 143:4

The psalmist wrote out these words, lamenting to God, showing the intense pain of a crushed heart. He knew that, even in the most excruciating spiritual pain, there was only one place to go for comfort: the loving heart of the Lord.

Meghan's first daughter was born with several disabling conditions. As a result, the baby would not be released from the hospital for several weeks. She would require surgery to stabilize her before her first day was over. Meghan spent every moment she could in the intensive care nursery with her child.

The next day, with the baby stable but in serious condition, Meghan checked out of the hospital alone. For years afterward she spoke with tear-filled eyes of the sensation she felt as she walked across the parking lot with her mother upon leaving the hospital.

It was the feeling of being empty. Her arms, which should have held a newborn baby, were empty. Her womb, having delivered its fruit, was empty. Her heart, which should have been bursting with joy, felt empty and dead.

Meghan turned in despair to God and was filled. She now speaks of how she never could have survived if it hadn't been for her relationship with a loving God.

I will never forget the haunted, empty eyes of a mother who stumbled past me in the intensive care unit of a large hospital where my son had just had surgery. I learned that both of her bright and beautiful daughters had been killed in a car accident by a drunk driver. I prayed for that mother and continued to do so for years.

I later found out that she had founded a Christian organization that came to the aid of mothers after the sudden loss of their children. The mother with the empty eyes had found her solace in God.

There is no one else to whom we can turn to fill that wounded place in our hearts.

Prayer: Lord, You alone are My strength. You alone can fill the emptiness that sometimes invades my spirit. Fill me now and give me hope.

He Despises No One

Behold, God is mighty, but despises no one.
—Job 36:5

There are days when you might feel abandoned by God. You may wonder if He even cares about you and your child anymore. You may even wonder if He hates you.

There may be myriad reasons for your thoughts. You may have done things in the past of which you need to repent. You may have thoughts that cause you guilt or shame. You may have times of anger toward God, toward others . . . toward your child.

As a result, you may think that you are the one person in this world whom God cannot love.

But we see the truth in Scripture that God hates no one. No one. That includes me. That includes you . . . no matter what. On the contrary, He loves you so much that if no one else in this world had ever existed, He would have endured the cross just for you!

He woos and pursues you with a patience that astounds. At times He may use our circumstances to shake us loose from whatever holds us back from a relationship with Him. He may allow what we see as misfortune to cause us pain in order to draw us back to Himself.

God does not hate you. He hates sin. He hates actions, but never the person committing them. Quite the contrary, He loves the person so much that He steps in and provides a way out of the eternal consequences for the actions.

You have not been abandoned. Search your life and see if the reason God may seem silent doesn't lie within you, wrapped in fear or anger or shame. Look deep within and bring what you find into the light of day, offering it to the Lord so that He can wipe it away and restore your relationship with Him.

Prayer: You are a loving God. Help me to accept Your love for me in the light of truth.

Yet I Will Trust Him   ✺

Though He slay me, yet will I trust Him.
—Job 13:15

Job had it all: a large family, a prosperous household, and a devout faith in God. But Job was brought to ruin and tested. He lost his family, his possessions, and his health. However, he never lost his faith in God. He knew that ultimately God would vindicate him, saving him from the snares of the devil.

There are many in this world who suffer without understanding, as Job did. Those of us with special-needs children may be tested daily. We bear the pain of watching our children struggle. We weep over their frustrations and physical pain.

How could anyone go through this without hope of restoration, without trust in a more knowing and merciful God?

Who else could ever give us the strength to endure, the rest needed to continue? Who else holds before us the promise of wholeness when we reach heaven? Where else in all the world can we find this kind of love and sacrifice on our behalf?

When we hang our heads in fear and despair, it is the very God of the universe who kneels before us, gathering us into His arms. He lifts our chins and wipes away our tears, gazing into our eyes, giving us His promise of eternity. He holds us and rocks us until the fears are quieted and hope is restored. He holds our hands and walks slowly beside us as we begin our journey again. He lifts the heavy load we carry, easing our burden.

And always before us is the vision of His eternal promise. There will be a day when our children will be whole. When we will never mourn their differences. When we will rejoice in the completeness of our souls.

Don't try to walk this road alone. It is far too difficult and painful. Invite Him to walk it with you. He will never leave you nor let you struggle in futility. He is the Friend you long for, the comfort you seek. He is the Lover of your soul.

Prayer: Lord, thank You for Your presence. Thank You that You care for me and my child. Thank You for Your steadfastness. Thank You for Your promise of restoration. Walk with me and be my Lord.

It's Not Fair!

Then Midianite traders passed by; so the brothers pulled Joseph up and lifted him out of the pit, and sold him to the Ishmaelites for twenty shekels of silver. And they took Joseph to Egypt.

—Genesis 37:28

Then Joseph's master took him and put him into the prison, a place where the king's prisoners were confined. And he was there in the prison.

—Genesis 39:20

"It's not fair!" I hear it from the lips of my children. I hear it resound in my own heart.

It's "not fair" that my twin sons are not allowed to have certain toys when their friends play with them. It's "not fair" that Kait cannot watch an R-rated movie in third grade when all of her closest friends have seen it. It's not fair that my girlfriend cannot conceive a child while another woman I know has had multiple abortions. It is not fair that our children have differences while others are whole.

It wasn't fair when Joseph was sold by his brothers because they were jealous of him. It wasn't fair that he was thrown into prison because his master's wife lied about him after she failed to seduce him. It wasn't fair that Joseph spent a long time in prison for a crime he did not commit. But Scripture shows no record of Joseph sinning or complaining.

When we read the story of Joseph in Genesis, we find that, because he was sold into Egypt, he met Potiphar, his master. During his time in Potiphar's household, he was propositioned by Potiphar's wife. Because Joseph did the right thing and fled from her, she called out to those in the household that Joseph had attacked her. He was thrown into prison. We find that, because he was in prison, he met someone who had had an unusual dream. Because God enabled Joseph to interpret the dream, this man remembered Joseph when the pharaoh had a disturbing dream. When he was able to help Pharaoh, through God's direction, Joseph became a powerful man. He was then able to save Egypt, and his family, from a seven-year famine.

God was using each of the "unfair" circumstances in Joseph's life to position him to do God's work. God had a plan for Joseph, and Joseph trusted God to bring it to fruition.

He will do the same for you. God has a plan for you and

your child. He is working to position you in order to bring His plan for your life to fruition.

This world is not fair. But God is; and, in the end, His justice is triumphant.

Prayer: Lord, Your ways are sometimes difficult. But we do not see from Your perspective. Help us to trust in the truth that You are just and righteous. You make a path for us no matter how difficult the journey.

Diversity

There are diversities of gifts, but the same Spirit. There are differences of ministries, but the same Lord. And there are diversities of activities, but it is the same God who works all in all. But the manifestation of the Spirit is given to each one for the profit of all.
—1 Corinthians 12:4–7

Quiana was born with problems. She required surgery shortly after delivery to correctly route her food and her air passages. Within a year her sister, Shayna, was born. Their mother tried to keep the girls on a similar developmental path.

Because of her differences, Quiana was unable to eat anything solid until she was three. Then her mother could cut a piece of cereal in half and allow her daughter to chew it carefully before swallowing it. Shayna was not allowed to eat anything solid until her sister could. Her mother was trying to spare Quiana some of the pain of being differently abled than her sister.

I wrestle with this issue too. I watch my eldest, a gifted singer and actress who has already gained extensive experience onstage. And I wonder whether her abilities will cause pain for Aiden, who has already struggled for years just to speak clearly.

I see hurt cross the face of my son as he watches his brother, a natural athlete. His twin is just a bit faster, just a little stronger, a half inch taller, and twenty-seven minutes older.

If we try to measure ourselves—or our children—against the achievements and abilities of others, we are sure to find disappointment. But God does not do this. He sees each person in her own right. He compares to no one. And we can help our children to do the same.

Show your child that everyone has his or her own special gifts from God. Michael Jordan is an incredible athlete. Luciano Pavarotti is a stupendous operatic tenor. Would it not be a waste of their talents and training if those two tried to switch places out of jealousy? Yet each has a place in the world that entertains millions.

Look for the unique attributes of your child. Does he have a cheerful nature? Does she have a forgiving spirit? Does your little one have a keen sense of beauty? Share what you find with your child. Explain that each of us has a unique place in God's plan for the world.

Our children don't have to be star singers or athletes to be special and wonderful. They are special and wonderful just as they are!

Prayer: Lord, You made my child in Your image, complete with inherent dignity and beauty. Help me to show my child the value You place in his or her life.

He Shall Not Be Hurt

He who has an ear, let him hear what the Spirit says to the churches. He who overcomes shall not be hurt by the second death.
—Revelation 2:11

As mothers of children with differences, we experience a type of pain that not everyone can understand.

One of the most difficult things for me in the first two years of Aiden's life was looking at little baby pouts. I have always loved the tender masterpiece of a baby's rosebud lips drawn into a full pout. I melt at the sparkling clear eyes, the upturned nose, the velvety dent below the nose leading to that cute pout.

But for those two years I averted my eyes. The sight of those little pouts caused a searing stab of pain deep within me, slashing at my heart. I was able to see the beauty of the baby before me, but I would also see the broken mouth of my son, the gaps in his lip and gums, the stitches, the scars. In time, the pain has faded to a dullness. I still feel a wistfulness at the sight of those "perfect" baby pouts. But I know my son is healthy, and to me he is beautiful.

It was difficult to explain to those around me how those little baby pouts affected me. But I found that every mother I spoke with, whether their child had differences or not, could relate to feeling pain. Everyone grieves. Everyone has hopes and dreams that go unfulfilled.

We will feel pain in this life. We will have loss. We will know sorrow. We will have struggles. But, in knowing Christ and through His grace, we are spared the greatest pain of all:

eternity without God . . . the eternal punishment of sinners . . . the second death.

On the contrary, we will move on to a place where pain will be no more. We will no longer suffer loss. We will never again feel sorrow. We will never struggle. Never again will we shed tears over our children. Our hopes and dreams will be reality.

And we will dwell in the house of the Lord forever.

Prayer: Lord, this present pain is only temporary. I look to the day that You will take away all pain and sorrow.

A Word of Encouragement

Exhort one another daily, while it is called "Today," lest any of you be hardened through the deceitfulness of sin.

—Hebrews 3:13

These words are written for you from mothers who have been where you are now—raising a child with differences, facing struggles, sorrow, and even the death of their children. Each is a message from one mother's heart to yours, in the name of Jesus, who is our comfort and our hope.

"Hold on to the hope—God sees your child, He knows your fears. He loves you more than you can ever comprehend!"

—Violet

"Everything that happens is filtered through His fingers. Trust in His goodness and wisdom. Hold on!"   —Joan

"God loves you. He is a God who forgives. At our weakest moment, He will forgive. The beautiful part is when He forgives, it's forgotten. So move on. Do your part . . ."

—Jackie

"Don't turn your back on God. Don't let your heart grow cold and hard. The struggles you face will be all the more difficult and painful if you go alone, without God's comfort and strength."

—Abigail

"Remember, you are never alone—there are thousands of us out there ready to help. And God is right there with you right now!"

—Lori

"This world is temporary. It is only a flicker in eternity. Look forward and see that you will have forever to dance with your child."

—Jennifer

"There is only one place to turn when your heart is breaking. Don't let your fear or anger or pride keep you from turning to Him."

—Pat

"Keep your chin up . . . it is easier to see heaven that way."

—Catherine

Dear mother, your baby is a precious and wonderful creation given to you by the King of kings, the Lord of all the universe.

You have been chosen over every woman in all of time to raise this special little one. The Lord has given you a great gift along with His promise to travel this journey at your side. Congratulations on the birth of your little one! May God bless you greatly in the years ahead.

—Carrie

This Grieving Savior

At the beginning of time, God created a beautiful and perfect world. There was no pain, no sorrow, no sin. He created two beautiful and perfect people to dwell in that world. These two people were made in the image of God Himself. They had a wondrous relationship with their Creator.

That is, until one dark day when they chose, of their own free will, to disobey God.

God had warned the two not to eat the fruit of a certain tree. A serpent spoke to the woman, convincing her to eat that forbidden fruit. She did so, knowing there would be consequences for her actions. She, in turn, offered the fruit to the man, and he ate it too.

From that day forward, a rift occurred between the people and the perfect God who created them. Sin entered the world. It was no longer perfect.

The serpent became the ruler of the world. His wrath at being less than God was played out upon the children of God. He caused brokenness and sickness. His desire was to destroy those whom God made in His image.

And so it is today. The problems you are experiencing are not directly caused by the hand of God. They are a part of this fallen world. And just as He wept at the grave of His friend Lazarus, so He weeps with you.

But in your pain, He offers you several gifts, the first of which is Himself.

When sin entered the world, a distance grew between the Creator, who is perfect, and His creation. God is holy, and no one who is sinful can stand in His presence throughout eternity.

And God is just. There are consequences for sin. There is eternal punishment.

However, God loves you so much that He made a special provision for that punishment. Knowing that no human being is without sin, God became a man and walked upon this earth. He took our sin on Himself and was put to death.

He took our punishment for us.

He now offers His sacrifice on our behalf as a free gift, which you can receive today—right now!

Below is a prayer. Read it over.

Father, I know I have sinned in my life. I am sorry for the sins I have committed. Please forgive me. But I also know that sin deserves punishment. You took my punishment upon Yourself, serving my sentence in my place. Today I receive that sacrifice on my behalf. I ask You to be my Savior and rule my heart. Thank You for the life You give me for all eternity. Amen.

Does this prayer speak to your heart? Go back and pray it with the knowledge that, once received, you now have forgiveness and eternal life. Best of all, you now enter into a special relationship with the God who created you, loves you, and lives in you.

The second gift God gives you is His Word, the Bible. In it

He writes His love letter to you. He offers you through His Word comfort, love, acceptance, wisdom, and growth.

His third gift is dialogue with Him—prayer. Pour out your heart to Him. He is big enough to handle your fear, your sorrow, your anger, and your joy. Then sit quietly and ask Him to fill you. Receive His peace and understanding, which He gives to you freely.